Front Runners

Front

More of the best o

London · 199

Runners

BROUGH SCOTT

Victor Gollancz Ltd

By the same author:

THE WORLD OF FLAT RACING
(with Gerry Cranham)

ON AND OFF THE RAILS

*Previous page: Racing at Newbury
(Chris Smith)*

ACKNOWLEDGEMENTS
These pieces originally appeared in the
Sunday Times, the *Independent on Sunday* and
Pacemaker magazine, to whom grateful thanks
are extended for permission to use them here.

Front Runners first published in
Great Britain 1991 by
Victor Gollancz Ltd,
14 Henrietta Street, London WC2E 8QJ

A CIP catalogue record is available from
the British Library.

ISBN 0-575-05207-4

Photoset by Rowland Phototypesetting Ltd,
Bury St Edmunds, Suffolk
Printed and bound in Great Britain by
Butler and Tanner Ltd, Frome, Somerset

Contents

List of Photographs

Prologue

In close, that's where the excitement, where the addiction lies. When the tapes go up, when the flag drops, when the whistle blows. When, suddenly, sport is all.

Many years ago I was there. Pretty bone-crunchingly badly some of the time, but nonetheless totally committed in body and soul to the challenge of making half a ton of steeplechaser shift itself quicker than any of its opponents.

For those eight seasons nothing else mattered one half as much. Not family, not friends, not the wider world, certainly not patient history tutors at Oxford, one of whom remained blissfully unaware of my racing time-out because he read the *Guardian* which in those sober days shielded its readers from reports of the Turf. Of course, it warped the mind and broke the body. And the "wasting" didn't do much for the digestion either. But it did take you to where there is no hiding place, where the judgements are swift and sometimes brutal. Where fools gather and hyenas call, where you have to face the consequences when the wolf can no longer make his kill.

Some see it as an escape, others as an aberration. In the global scheme of things that is of course correct. But close up, sport has its own reality, and a raw, direct appeal that works right across the spectrum and down the ages. That's what I searched for once, and what I seek in others now.

The pieces assembled here are from the *Sunday Times*, the *Independent on Sunday* and, in one case, from *Pacemaker Magazine*. They start where my last collection, *On and Off the Rails*, left off in May 1984. The main criterion for inclusion is that what hit me then should still affect me now. Except for the odd literal correction, they remain as they were written. They are a record of how things were for this set of eyes and ears, hands and feet.

The parish may seem a narrow one, but it stretches around the globe. We've been to Australia, Japan, America and Africa as well as all across the European track. And we also touch wider fields—not just a dozen other sports, but some places where no one can remain detached.

They may be names on the map. Who can be indifferent to Northern Ireland, to East Berlin, indeed to Soweto? But they are most often places within. Those elements of strength and weakness, fire and water, which make up the actors on the racing and the sporting scene. How they handle the cards which fate, physique and fitness deal them remains the eternal fascination of any game right through to life itself.

These pieces and this book could not have been put together without a heck of a lot of support. To have worked in harness with photographers like Chris Smith and now Norman Lomax has been an education. Many times have I sat at the desk staring at a Chris Smith picture and thought "That's worth at least three thousand words—I might as well go home!"

Previous page: Bumpy ride. Jonjo O'Neill (left) in a spot of bother in his riding days (Chris Smith)

Sports Editors who wait for my copy tend to grow old before their time, so it's important to honour: David Robson, John Lovesey and Chris Nawrat of the *Sunday Times*, and Richard Williams and Simon O'Hagan at the *Independent on Sunday*, for patience as well as pressure.

Other colleagues have almost as bad a deal. Andrew Franklin at Channel 4 has been generous way beyond the call of duty. Michael Harris at *Racing Post* knows the symptoms and understands. Cherry Forbes, at whatever desk, car or plane filled in as the office, has been a rock which never crumbled. Joanna Goldsworthy at Gollancz has, incredibly, been going through these hoops a second time.

To all of them, and to all of you who read this book, thanks for coming with me. It's been quite a journey. And we have only just begun.

1. The Dream and Its Dangers

*Always the double-edged sword, the pleasure is quick
but so too is the pain. Entering the racing world is
sport's version of* Through the Looking Glass.
*Everything looks different in there, feels different.
By turns absurd, glorious, funny and sad. But held
together by a strange connecting four-legged thread. It
has dragged this Alice all over the place.*

*First a bigger bump than you ever get in fairy
tales.*

My Aintree nightmare
March 24th 1985

Every life has a waking dream that turns into nightmare. Mine happened
exactly 20 years ago next Saturday. It was called the Grand National.

Distance is supposed to lend enchantment. Aintree memories are meant
to be of heroic days and joshing nights, and when tackled about any pre-race
nerves our hero gives a B-movie laugh and says: "Well there were a few
butterflies in the changing-room, but once we were out for the race everything was great." Not here it wasn't.

Mind you, everybody was very nice to the still pretty innocent Mr B Scott
—the other jockeys, the tough but kindly "Frenchy" Nicholson as he legged
me up, stable lad Barry Davies as he led us out on to the track and even
big, thundering Time as he plodded beneath me during the parade.

But the problems now were quite appallingly obvious. All those runners
(there were no fewer than 56 that year) over those all-too-famous Grand
National fences (the obligatory on-foot inspection had been no comfort);
and on this horse. Time was a huge, tough old sod, and we'd been through
a fairly encouraging run at Cheltenham a fortnight earlier. But the year
before, when National favourite, he had kept landing too heavily in the
drops, and the idea today was to go more gently, to let him "fiddle" round,
to (oh happy phrase!) "keep out of trouble".

Well, Julius Caesar might have liked having fat men around him for
reassurance, but the trick at the start of the National is to get beside someone lean and hungry who looks as if they know what they are doing. But
just as we got jammed in next to crack jockeys Bill Rees and David Nicholson, old Time contrarily backed out of line, the space was taken and when
we finally got back in it was between two nervous looking amateurs, one
of whom, Chris Collins, had wasted so deathly white that I remember giving
him last words of unneeded support. He eventually finished third, I ended
up in Walton hospital.

Maybe I had read too much Siegfried Sassoon about war in the trenches,

*Overleaf: Peter
Walwyn's string
exercising at
Lambourn (Chris
Smith)*

but the parallel here had just about everything save the Flanders mud. The long, stamping, cursing line was the "stand to". The starter's shout and the tapes flying up was "over the top". The grit of the Melling Road was "through the wire into no man's land". The long row of fences up ahead were the enemy lines.

And we were straightaway in trouble. Off his legs and at the back of the field, Time landed deep in the drop at the first, and all the way down to Becher's it was a horrible, scrambling struggle to stay in one piece.

We could never get any rhythm, find any passage. There were loose horses everywhere, and even the mounted cavalry were all over the place. A grey horse kept coming leftwards into me. At the fifth fence I'd seemed to have escaped him. The next was Becher's; you could hear the commentary and see the crowds on the far side. Two strides off it, the grey horse came slap across us. For a dreadful doomed moment we blundered completely blind into the fence of fences.

Even in hell you can have moments of love. I loved Time then. For somehow he got over Becher's, survived the steep, steep landing, bulldozed past two fallers and suddenly the first smoke of horror had cleared.

In other days. Brough Scott and John Oaksey battle it out in the saddle rather than the commentary box

Chesterton's donkey might have had his hour "one far, fierce hour and sweet". Time and I only had about four minutes. But as the fences began to flick by below us, and we began actually to make contact with this race, this Grand National, we had our moment, everything except the palms beneath our feet.

But nightmare, albeit of a simpler kind, was waiting. Going out for the second circuit, Time was steaming along so strongly that the 30 lengths we were off the leaders seemed no great gap. Confidence was growing, but carelessness was close. At the big ditch, I sat still, indecisive. Time galloped slap into it, somersaulted high and heavy, and then I was in the ambulance with the Duke of Alburquerque.

The pay-off put things into perspective. The ambulance went from fence to fence, and stretcher parties brought across the wounded. Eventually we headed back to the racecourse doctor, on to hospital and presumably to anxious orderlies all ready to greet and tend their heroes.

Well, poor Jimmy Morrissey was rushed in to have his smashed head treated. The old duke was put behind a curtain, where he mystified the assembled medics by moaning, "Mon genou, mon genou." But the other two of us, still in breeches, boots and grass-stained jockey sweaters, just sat on the bench next to the granny who had tripped over on the pavement, and the little boy who had cut his hand on a milk bottle.

Eventually a polite little doctor called us forward. The broken collarbone was not difficult to diagnose, but the cause of the accident appeared to be beyond him. "What have you been doing?" he asked. "At what races? How long ago?" Maybe it was a dream after all.

However hard the breaks and bruises feel at the time, in hindsight they were nothing but a bonus. A "searing-in" of the experience, the dues you pay to be one of the fraternity, the entry fee for unique access long after the boots are hung up and the saddles given away.

The invitations to what seem like Mad-Hatters' Tea Parties have seen some magic moments. Who could refuse an Irish one in France?

An Irish mare becomes queen of France
June 24th 1984

History should never be as nice. On Friday in Paris, Dawn Run became the first horse ever to land the clean sweep of Champion Hurdles, the Irish, English and now the French. She also did something more important. She and her happy little team from County Kilkenny proved that it is still possible to scale the highest of sporting peaks without fuss, and with a smile.

This was a performance to which all the human delights and equestrian achievements of Royal Ascot must bow. A start-to-finish six-length thrashing of the world's richest and best-bred hurdlers in a time of 6min 2sec for the 5,100 metres (three miles one-and-a-half furlongs). "That's going one minute ten seconds to the kilometre," said one awe-struck local observer. "She's the best we have seen in twenty years. *Un phénomène.*"

But the charm and the cunning of the Irish way is that a top horse remains as much a chum as a champion. So it was that the night before's after-dinner schedule included a trip down the leafy suburban avenues of Maisons-Laffitte, and an expectant pad across the stable-yard, to slide back the bolt on the favourite for the big race on the morrow. "Isn't she after looking in marvellous fettle?" whispered Dawn Run's chief attendant, Jim Murphy, when he had given the great, gleaming Amazon her midnight bowl of oats. "I honestly think we have never had her better."

Only a stony heart would not be melted by the heady belief inherent in such a nocturnal pilgrimage, but with the morning came the doubts. The old mare looked something of a milk horse compared with the flashy little French "mokes" already out *en promenade*.

Murphy, and trainer Paddy Mullins's two sons, Tony and Tom, were wide-eyed yokels in this sophisticated suburb, which is to Paris what Richmond is to London. Worse still, "the boys" were about to launch Dawn Run on a limbering-up session which seemed to defy the present state of the training art.

On the morning of a race, most trainers now take the view that their athlete needs no more priming than the canter he will get on his way to the start. Indeed, Vincent O'Brien's El Gran Senor never broke a walk in the two days prior to the Derby, or before his winning run in the Two Thousand Guineas. Yet here was Dawn Run's jockey, Tony Mullins, smoking merrily away in the saddle, doing a 50-minute exercise on race morning, including a canter and a full-pace jumping "school".

"Jaysus, didn't she lep?" yelled Tony as he brought Dawn Run back after the second hurdle. "I've never known her as keen as this." Mullins has a thin, pointed, pale face which cracks into a lovely youthful smile. Like all the Mullins family, he's a skilled horseman who has been riding since the dummy came out of his mouth. Yet Tony's only 22, Tom 20. And with Jim Murphy a veteran of 26, the doubter was bound to remember that Tony had only regained the ride on Dawn Run from the injured Jonjo O'Neill in April, and to wonder whether this cheery non-French-speaking trio weren't boys in a man's world.

Most of these doubts were dispelled by the arrival of "the man himself". Paddy Mullins is not given to hearty, hail-fellow-well-met entrances, and now at one moment Tony and Tom were hosing down Dawn Run after exercise, the next Paddy Mullins was standing beside her, his shoulders hunched, eyes alert like the lean, silver-haired specialist he is. Mullins checked the mare's eyes, legs, feet, shoes, listened to the boys, and then came quietly over and said: "I think she is in rare form."

At times like this you appreciate where Paddy's more outgoing sons, and indeed his horses, got their inner confidence. So while Tony, in new suit, still looked a bit rustic as we drove the dozen kilometres into Paris and off into the Bois de Boulogne for Auteuil, he also sounded happily reassuring. "I don't get tense beforehand, but I do afterwards when I think what was at stake," he said candidly. "Anyway," he added later, as he enlivened our walk round France's premier jumping track (like Cheltenham in SW1) by leaping on top and over the hurdles himself, "I've had my fall for the week, at Roscommon on Tuesday night. It was like the road. This watered ground is a carpet in comparison. I think the mare will be all right."

The race itself was simple. By the time the big mare reached the first of these wider and stiffer French hurdles, she was clocking something much quicker than 1:10 to the kilometre. By the time she got round the first bend, she was out on her own. Two great laps of the track, and the nearest rivals closed to within four lengths on the final turn, but once into the straight it was all too obvious that she had run them ragged.

Dawn Run in action is more thundering powerhouse than elegant oil-painting. But as owner Charmian Hill greeted an ecstatic Tony Mullins afterwards ("I had a lot left in the tank, ma'am") to the French cries of "bravo!", as Paddy Mullins anxiously checked the mare over afterwards for lameness in the left shoulder, you realised what is so attractive about her. It is simply that Dawn Run's style, like that of those around her, puts the heart out in front.

But you can't win 'em all. Touting around the racing parish can soon fill you with self-importance. It's not a quality that travels very well. Especially not to the other side of the Atlantic. Witness this confession from the first Breeders' Cup Day, dateline Los Angeles, November 1984.

I was a Hollywood also-ran
November 18th 1984

Hollywood, and not just Hollywood Park, should have been my oyster. There I was in California for Breeders' Cup Day, dressed up in an NBC TV blazer and masquerading as an English racing expert with the built-in advantage that there was hardly another Englishman around. And I still blew it . . .

This was the chance to chalk up all those invitations to Beverly Hills, become a friend of the famous. But the trick is to know the people as well as the horses. For instance, when that familiar-looking silver-haired man came up chatting about English racing, it was a shade unwise to give him the brush-off usually reserved for TV tip-touters without realising he was John Forsyth, Blake Carrington of "Dynasty". More than unwise, perhaps, for the genial Forsyth is a high-powered horse-owner newly elected to racing's Hall of Fame. And the sun-tanned blonde over there by the cheese . . . surely that wasn't Linda Evans?

The trouble with getting locked into the horse barns as a racing correspondent is that you are apt to behave like a bow-legged buffoon when you get out into the Grandstand, or in Hollywood Park's case (for a mere $80) to the Pavilion of the Stars. Only an oats-fed oaf would have turned down an invitation to the gala evening on the grounds that such occasions are usually non-events. This one turned out to have Frank Sinatra live on stage for only 200 people.

Oh yes, and the dumpy little lady going to the TV table just happened to be Liz Taylor (she's quite difficult to recognise from behind).

At other race meetings, you have just-as-exotically dressed, albeit absolutely anonymous, creatures in the chairman's box. But only at Hollywood Park would they actually be "Ol' Blue Eyes" or the face that has launched a thousand ships (and several husbands). And there was Cary Grant looking out with the pride of a director of this racetrack, originally the brainchild of the "Old Groaner", Bing Crosby. Even Fred Astaire was there, much too frail to dance these days, but still able to pull out a wry line under pressure.

Fred's wife, ex-jockey Robyn Smith, was a mounted part of our four-hour TV marathon which for all its so-so ratings of 5.1 (20 million viewers) against 6.0 and 8.1 for two grid-iron football games, was the biggest attempt yet at putting the whole hyped-up absurdity of a great racing day on to the screen.

The snag for the purist was that there were quite a few more human stars than equine ones; and that's not just sour grapes for the eclipse of Lear Fan. True, the filly Princess Rooney looked a real smasher, and the two-year-old Chief's Crown would probably take any of our colts to the cleaners if they were dumb enough to tackle him on the dirt. But otherwise, apart from wondering how many winners would actually pass a European dope test (even the world record-breaker, Royal Heroine, was on Lasix), the highspot of the day was the excitement of the Stewards' inquiries.

Now in Britain, from Admiral Rous's day down to these over-exposed TV times, the Stewards' inquiry is one of the few processes of justice to remain behind closed doors. Not so in the sunshine state. After the second race on Saturday, a grizzled old Chilean jock named Fernando Toro came rushing up to the TV post, seized a phone at our feet and called up the Stewards high on the roof to complain bitterly about the winner's steering off the final turn.

"He justah comah out and killah me," said Fernando, to the enlightenment not just of the officials but of the TV audience, who could see not only Toro in full flood, but the inquiry room itself, with shirt-sleeved worthies peering at the re-runs. In the final Breeders' Cup race things were even better. A three-way bumping match, three frantic telephone calls . . . and there were the Stewards having to take the most public ever scrutiny of what, at $3m, had been the richest race ever run. Try that on the Rowley Mile.

If the backwoodsmen would have been shaken by some of this, those with a disciplinary bent would surely have approved of one closing scene at the horse barn on Sunday morning. As Lashkari, winner of the $2m Turf race for the Aga Khan, walked round with his lad, some cautious soul had suggested a little security to avoid any repetition of the Shergar episode. Two largish, casually dressed gentlemen duly appeared, and a punctilious colleague asked if they were armed. One of the guys let his coat fall open to reveal an impressive firearm obviously capable of dealing with anything short of the Manson family. He gave us limey losers a contemptuous look, and said "Yeah". We didn't make friends with him either.

Would that self-inflicted foul-ups were confined to professional life. In the Scott family it hasn't been necessarily so. Come the winter they get the call of the mountains. I keep failing to avoid it. Here's a desperate SOS from the loneliness of a mid-morning cable car, rendezvous for a reject.

As a skier my guttering candle is barely alight
January 10th 1988

This year's disaster was the boots. We had reached the eighth day of the skiing holiday. Once again humiliation had got its man.

Marrying a lady who had done avalanche patrol in the Rockies was always going to present problems for this non-skier. But 14 years on we surely reached the nadir on Wednesday. The third child bombed confidently down the nursery slope, looked back at the inadequate slitherings of his sire, and called: "Come on, Dad. Have a try. It's not that difficult."

Dammit, I have tried and it's still difficult. Over the years it seems that I have been dragged up almost every icy mountain, plunged down every rushy glen that the Alps has to offer. A litany of names even a ski-bum would envy. But disaster, usually self-inflicted, was never far behind.

There was the first shattering, black-bruised attempt in Zermatt. There was fog in Flaine, a giant blister in Verbier, a rock at Val d'Isère, a twisted ankle at Meribel, and a faulty T-bar at Zurs which cut out with me and a giant German dangling from a blizzard-swept precipice like two pieces of rapidly freezing meat.

Worst of all was Avoriaz, the first trip *en famille*. Despite living in what appeared to be a cupboard, the five of us got on so passably well that in the departure lounge at Geneva Airport I was idiot enough to say: "At least nothing major has gone wrong this time."

You'll never believe this, but at that moment a pain started in my chest which, by the time the plane was taxi-ing for take-off, seemed to be the crushing force of the Great Reaper himself. My last words, unoriginally, were: "Take care of the children." The plane was stopped and a flashing ambulance blue-lighted me to intensive care.

The fact that the most comprehensive cardiac tests ever devised only suggested a virus which could be cured by aspirin meant that the "Blighty wound" that would end all skiing holidays had yet to arrive. Four winters on and we're still at it. This time it's Klosters.

This unique little town just 20km (12 miles) from Davos in the eastern end of Switzerland has won recent renown as "the royal resort". Each February a shivering group of paparazzi are made to appreciate a printable truth about the Prince of Wales. While it may or may not be true that Prince Charles has deep and meaningful conversations with the Highgrove cabbages, he's about as far from being a wimp as a mountain can measure. If you doubt that, try the eight-mile, 6,000ft descent, as he has, from Weiss-fluhjoch to Kublis in 14 minutes.

Only a junior royal was around last week, but there was a much bigger problem. It appears that Klosters is my wife's second home. They call out her name in the ski shop, at the restaurants and of course all sorts of swooping latter-day Killys echo it across the mountain. The need to be more than the usual embarrassing, craven consort becomes acute.

Down the seasons she has gallantly tried every way of giving help—by turns being kind, harsh, instructional, even dismissive. Nowadays, despite countless memories of wrenching myself down impossible slopes after her nimble, skipping bottom, there has to be a degree of resignation about our skiing relationship. Entry to that magic powder-snow land of high mountain shoulders, wild spaces, and vertigo-steep gullies still looks a world away.

Yet this time things had started rather well. We had almost the only white spot in the Alps, the best first day ever, all kit comfortable, family happy, the skiing not too strange.

By day two we had even completed a slightly sozzled New Year's race.

Lady Scott wound the clock back in style but at least I finished ahead of *The Times* racing correspondent. A tiny step can be a dangerous thing and, too emboldened, I went back to the course on my own, somersaulted, bloodied the nose, and something began to go wrong with the boots.

At first it was just a soreness around the shin. Then the whole foot seemed to hurt, the ski didn't relate to the leg. The incomparable Hans Hartmann's shop produced a new boot. That hurt even more, and by now we were into an all-too-familiar saga—down the plughole of self-pity into the exhaustion of defeat.

Since then one or two turns with a now-corrected boot and one sublime fresh snow morning have kept hope's guttering candle just alight. But we should record that Siggi in the ski shop took a more gloomy view. "Perhaps," he said with plenty of mountain wisdom in his laugh, "you only have two answers. Change ze sport, or change ze wife."

Somehow the Scott family soldiers on. We all will if we can still steal a smile out of life. But it's not always easy. It wasn't in Lambourn as the leaves turned in 1988.

Hope still beats in Lambourn's village heart
September 4th 1988

Nothing could have looked more blessed. The village, the church, the string of horses trotting high on to the Downs above. But remember the past month and you could really believe there was a curse upon the land.

We often talk of sports being beleaguered. We mean they are entrammelled in scandal, failure, hooliganism or some other man-made disaster. The little world of horse racing has its share of all that, but over the past few weeks it has had a rather bigger problem. Three young people have died and two other crashes have proved nearly fatal. It seems to have been beset by fate.

Normally these things come in one single, shattering catastrophe. A road accident to the team bus, the dreadful air disaster that hit the Busby Babes in 1958, the Olympics killings in the same city of Munich in 1972. For racing, and in particular for the little Berkshire village of Lambourn where those horses were trotting on Friday morning, the hurt has come in much smaller but unforgivingly repeated drops.

At this stage you should appreciate that horse racing can be at the same time the purest and yet most bogus of sporting activities. Bogus, because it encourages, via gambling, millions to get involved who haven't the remotest notion of what the actual physical game is about. But pure because once committed to the actual horse side you have joined more than a fellowship, you are part of a family.

Sure, it's as disparate, wrangling and divisive a group as you could find. Yet, once hooked, its members hardly ever leave, and tend to adopt a language, lifestyle, even a geography of their own. Manchester becomes a place 20 miles east of Haydock, Glasgow is just north of Hamilton, Portsmouth 10 miles south-west of Goodwood.

In this world Lambourn, a little valley village of barely 3,000 souls, looms like a metropolis second only to Newmarket, the capital of the world. Everyone has been to Lambourn, most have worked in one of the yards there at some time or other.

Wherever they live, racing people are all as interlinked and interbred as the 1,000-odd horses clattering around the Lambourn lanes on Friday morning. So this sleepy haven, just beginning to stir to the problems of dormitory-town planning and the advance of Yuppiedom, is entitled to think of everyone in the game as one of its own.

Into this community fate has lobbed five hand grenades of misfortune over the past month. There was the death of Paul Croucher, a favourite son and a jump jockey of championship calibre, in a car crash on the Faringdon Road. Susan Piggott (Lester was brought up in Lambourn) and Steve Cauthen (he still has a house in the village) both shaved death in terrible riding accidents. Not so lucky were Carmel Roche and Vivian Kennedy, whose young lives were snuffed out last week.

"We seem to have had it up to here," said the lad riding beside me on Friday. Paul, Carmel and Vivian would all have been people he mixed with every day. Car-driving, which had also claimed Carmel, and race-riding, which ended so tragically for Vivian Kennedy after his fall at Huntingdon last Monday, would be two of the central pleasures of his existence. You might have expected a pall of sorrow to hang over him, just as it had over the unhappy people of nearby Hungerford after the macabre massacre there in August last year.

But it was not so. For racing, more than almost any other activity, offers a daily chance of renewal. The horses have to go out, and as you feel them strong beneath you, they demand the belief that winners and good days can return.

The string reached the top of the ridge and filed back past us. One of the wind-blown riders suddenly looked familiar. It was Tanya Davis, Paul Croucher's strikingly pretty girlfriend, a fine jockey herself.

They had been a couple made in dreams. There were no words to say. Way below us, the sun dappled bright on the churchyard. It was a grand morning. In her smile there was only a hint of sadness. For Tanya knows, as we all should know, that even in the blackest times there has to be hope amongst the hoofbeats.

*Death in the community seems to blacken out the sun,
and sometimes a wider perspective is needed to clear
the darkness. At the start of the nineties even the racing
world couldn't stay immune to the astonishing events
in Eastern Europe. Indeed, what was happening on
the turf just outside Berlin was so vivid a microcosm of
the whole East–West impasse that BBC radio
commissioned a horseback version for their Eurofile
series, complete with bumping, breathless
sound-effects from this saddle-sore presenter.*

East meets West at the races
March 25th 1990

The lights are going on all over Europe and some fine old relics are emerging from the dark. But with them comes the harshest of realities: can you revive past glories after years in the unthinking cupboards of Communism?

Artur Böhlke, the head of East German racing, has to hope so. For next Saturday's first all-German meeting in 29 years at East Berlin's historic Hoppegarten track isn't just a gamble, it is everything.

"I am like the man playing roulette," Böhlke said on Monday afternoon as the enormity of the election results began to sink in. "I have to take all my chips and back just one number."

Next Saturday will be Hoppegarten's biggest deal since Hitler played the loser, and if it can't draw new support and investment from the West, the place which for so long ranked with Newmarket and Chantilly will also be for the history books.

"We are entirely state-owned," said Böhlke, who was born at Hoppegarten 51 years ago. "So we depend almost completely on a subsidy of 13 million marks to pay all the wages and costs of keeping our five racecourses and five national studs afloat. I have been told that this subsidy will not continue."

A crowd of 35,000 (twice the post-war record) is expected at the weekend, many of them West Berliners making the 10-mile trip east from the old capital just as their forebears did to see the Kaiser race in the imperial days and, later, to gaze in trapped fascination when Goering flaunted his extravagant uniforms in the winners' circle.

But most of Saturday's visitors will travel only out of one-off curiosity. Böhlke's roulette throw is to persuade enough of them that a new age is worth pursuing.

As relics go, Hoppegarten still shows plenty signs of life. There may be blotchy holes of neglect in the sand tracks but the 4,000-acre training centre remains larger than anything in West Germany and still evokes thoughts of Newmarket, on which it was modelled in the 1860s. There may be rusty railings and peeling masonry but the sweep and size of the racecourse still has the grandeur of central Europe's finest stage.

At first sight you could think that one massive dollop of filthy capitalism and the whole place might be in shape again. But it's a lot more difficult than that. Long before you get round to wondering whether a new, united, Berlin-centred Germany will have either the cash or the inclination to play the punter, you have to refashion the game itself.

"It's no good just blaming Honecker and the other comrades," says Böhlke, who was never a party member and, surprise, surprise, didn't get his present title until the week after the Berlin Wall came down. "Racing itself has a lot to answer for. It always resisted restructuring, had far too many people employed, and didn't make success a criterion."

Admittedly, the money is very poor. Exchange rates claim parity to the

Artur Böhlke in front of the stand at Hoppegarten. Like the jockey on the right (B. Scott), it has clearly seen better days (Chris Smith)

West German mark (2.6 to the pound) but the black market has it five times as weak. So there's not much reward in the state's wages for a stable lad on 700 marks a month, trainers and jockeys on 800 marks plus 4 per cent of winnings, and Böhlke, the head of the whole shooting match, on just 1,600 marks.

Yet there is a certain cosy comfort amid the drabness. Every lad keeps his job, however lazy, and each of Hoppegarten's 20 trainers keeps his allotted 20 horses, however unsuccessful. And, most ludicrous of all, the studs get a guaranteed 29,000-mark payment for each of the 170 yearlings transferred in the autumn, however poor the individuals.

"It will be a painful process but everything will have to change," says Böhlke. "The trainers will no longer be employees of the state, and we will not be able to buy their horses for them, or provide them with supplies of hay and oats from the co-operative farm. They will have to adapt to independence and the need to attract customers."

On the face of it this seems an impossible order but already there is a certain crinkle-eyed, out-of-the-abyss optimism about Böhlke. "Things will get worse before they get better," he says. "But the election result means that unity will come sooner rather than later. Berlin will be capital of Germany once more. Before the war, Hoppegarten had 1,500 horses. Those days could come again."

But quite horrendous obstacles remain. Apart from the likelihood of a traffic jam stretching straight back to the Brandenburg Gate, there are appalling logistical problems; with toilet arrangements, with the specially borrowed West German tote machines which will operate in the two currencies, and with the small matter of who actually owns the racecourse.

Imagine if the Russians had overrun the south of England in 1945 and "Free Britain" was racing horses at Newmarket for the first time next Saturday. Would the Jockey Club lay claim again to its original creation? "Everything is up in the air," says Böhlke, "but we will be discussing it next week. We will certainly need their help."

Böhlke, whose uncle Eric was one of the country's finest jockeys, has got Mercedes Benz and *Bild*, Germany's largest-circulation paper, as main sponsors. He has invited the great and good from Britain and France as well as every German politician and industrialist he can muster. In earlier life he worked in banking and as a state bookie but he has always burned for Hoppegarten.

On the human side he will not lack support. It might not be so easy for the horses. East German animals are rated so inferior to their West German counterparts that they will be receiving 10 to 14 kilos in the handicaps. Since West German horses are a good seven kilos behind British runners, this puts the Hoppegarten locals in the donkey class.

As part of our fact-finding tour I was loaded up on a handsome, well-turned-out four-year-old who rejoiced in the name of Socrates. As we galloped easily across the training grounds, it was an unhappy thought that unless Socrates and his fellows concentrate their minds wonderfully they are odds-on to meet the same fate as the brilliant German Derby winner, Alchimist. In 1945 his flight to safety was overtaken by starving Russian troops.

Forty-five years on, reality and a racing renaissance may have to start with the dinner plate.

Sadly that last prediction turned out to be all too true. The "Reunification Race Meeting" was an unbelievable success, 50,000 people, fiesta in the air, the opening event won by jockey Lutz Mader on his first visit to Hoppegarten since he fled East Germany by swimming the Oder 20 years before. But the local horses were never sighted. Bloodlines as well as financial backing will all have to come from the West.

Let's go further afield now, across the Atlantic to Monmouth Park, New Jersey, to share a day with a 22-carat phenomenon. There are plenty of words here. The subject demands them.

Flying feathers behind the mane
September 9th 1990

She must be the smallest history-maker since Admiral Nelson. She's still got both her eyes but nearly lost an arm last year. This week she has come back to the big time. New York welcomes Julie Krone.

At 4ft 10in and barely 7st she's a midget even in the Lilliputian world of the jockeys' room. But her achievement is colossal. For massed against her was something as formidable as the French fleet at Trafalgar—all those centuries of male supremacy.

Everyone knew that a woman couldn't ride racehorses like a man. Show jumping, dressage and three-day eventing may have yielded marvellously to the tender touch, but race-riding; stick-up, head-down, arms-pumping, full battle on horseback; that was too tough. It would always be man's work.

It used to be against the law. Kathy Kusner had to take the Americans to court in 1968. Linda Jones did the same in Australia 10 years later. Britain gave in more meekly. But after the first triumphant fanfares of feminism the statistics began to repeat the old refrain. There were some quick sensations but no woman lasted anywhere near the top level. They couldn't really compete.

Until Julie Krone.

Even now you have to read the records to believe it. Her first winner came at Florida's Tampa Bay Downs in February 1980. Nobody thought her anything more than another horse-mad 16-year-old set for imminent obscurity. Yet by the end of the decade there had been 1,897 extra trips to the winners' circle and she had led the rankings at Monmouth Park and at New York's Meadowlands for the last three seasons.

In 1989 she was fourth in the all-American table with 368 winners and $8m (£4.2m) in prize money. Remember that Pat Eddery topped the English list with 171 winners and £2.3m last year, and you realise that Krone is into very big bucks indeed.

Over here we still couldn't really swallow it. In France only gallant little Caroline Lee flies the flag for the women. In England today only Alex Greaves and Kim Tinkler feature in the top 60 and they have each landed just a dozen winners on the turf this summer. America must be an easier game, and anyway from what we have been told Krone was something of a fighting cat.

Years ago she knocked Yves Turcotte off the scales at Pimlico, had to be torn apart from Jake Nied at Keystone, got busted for drugs at Bowie, and at Monmouth Park got fined $100 for smashing Miguel Rujano over the head with a deck chair after he had pushed her into the jockeys' swimming pool. So the girl could look after herself. But after last November wasn't the whole thing over?

For that night at the Meadowlands Krone got the sort of fall the pessimists had predicted. A stricken horse pitched down on her, a following one finished the job. It took four and a half hours of surgery to save her left arm and after another three months the injury needed a bone graft from the hip.

The old clouds rolled back. Women couldn't survive the brutal side of the business. The new decade would need a fresh beginning. Krone couldn't even start until July 25th. Monmouth Park, just off the Atlantic shore in New Jersey, where a century ago such swells as "Diamond Jim" Brady, Lily Langtry and that splendidly named American president Ulysses S Grant, stepped out in their finery. Krone was only in jockey's silks, but she tossed her whip back as a winner. Krone was a name again.

Opposite: Julie Krone—racing's own version of Wonderwoman (Heinz Kluetmeier/ Sports Illustrated/ Colorific)

In the five weeks that followed she had ridden 40 more winners, 10 ahead of any other pilot on the grounds. This was the place where she had made her reputation. Last week it seemed a good spot to check her out. Even at 6.30 on a Friday morning. She wasn't hard to find. She was outside the stable area on the "backstretch", sitting on a golf buggy with her long-time agent Larry Cooper who, by reason of his charming, slithery insistence, has

always been known as "Snake". She was easily identifiable because she had a pink helmet cover with "Julie Krone" on the back. But the sight of her was a shock. This wasn't some great butch fighting cat. This was Tweetie Pie.

It is always an effort for us to fit a giant reputation into a tiny physique. With jockeys it is not unusual. Shoemaker, Saint-Martin, even Carson. But Julie Krone was an extra dimension. The figure on that golf buggy, moving between the spreading beech trees and the green canvas barns of Monmouth Park's 1,500-horse hostel, was absolutely tiny.

But you wouldn't say coy or petite. She may be the size of Walt Disney's famous canary but she is also every bit as lively. She's Julie Krone. Suddenly she breaks away from conversation and shouts "Hey, Willie." She is talking to a horse.

Now lots of riders have, or affect, a matey relationship with the four-legged athletes on whom they earn their corn. There is plenty of slapping of the neck and "hello big fella". But with Krone it was different. It was as if a favourite dog, albeit a massive, saddled and ridden one, had come round the corner. Julie rushed up to it. What else could the horse do? He stopped to talk.

His real name was Master Speaker. He and Julie had won a big race last year. "He's so cute the way he looks at you," she said. "He knows he's out here to do something important but he doesn't get fired up until you take him away to work."

Child-like it may be, but this lack of inhibition makes communication refreshingly direct with humans as well as horses. "Gee, I was so excited I couldn't sleep last night," she confides. Not, you'll be surprised to hear, at the prospect of meeting us, but because she had been booked to "breeze" top sprinter Safely Kept at 6a.m. "She's a real race mare," says Krone. "I kept thinking of her in full stride and man I was not disappointed this morning. Let's go and see her over here."

We were all jammed in the front seat of the buggy, but Snake drove us imperiously past the usual sweeping brooms and hosing horses of the American backstretch to let us dismount and risk life and limb by getting into the stall with the largest female athlete this side of the hippo cage. Safely Kept has almost carthorse dimensions and seeing her standing there with our little canary twittering around her was to realise the scale of the physical role that Krone accomplishes in the saddle.

By now it is not only second nature to her, it is accepted by the hardened professionals around the lot. As she talks of the thrill of riding a "class" horse like Safely Kept—"When she hits her stride, you feel the power come flooding up beneath you"—Larry Cooper is already into other bookings for the trainer, manoeuvring his jockey into live mounts for next week when the racing circus moves up to its base at the Meadowlands racetrack just next to where the New York Giants play American football.

"Yeah," said Snake in that laid-back Maryland drawl. "Everything is in gear. She's riding good, the trainers are pretty receptive, we have a lot of business. We've been together eight years now. That's longer than most marriages. What she has done is unbelievable—third or fourth on the list for the last two years—to do that in a man's world is incredible. It's like a girl playing short stop for the Yankees."

The relationship which has remained strictly professional and has survived injury, suspension, hard times and Krone's change of boyfriend, only happened by chance. "I was down at Atlantic City and another agent asked me to take Julie until he arrived. He never showed up and here we are."

Cooper had never managed a woman rider before but soon began to notice that here was something unusual. "There was plenty of prejudice originally, trainers saying 'my owner won't ride a girl'. There was this one trainer in particular, Tommy Green. He never even had a girl working in the shed room. That's how he was brought up. You know, the 'Old South'. By the middle of the meet we were first call for him. Even so, he kept saying 'I can't believe I am riding a girl. It's just beyond me.'"

The key to all this has to lie on the racetrack. All Julie's bounce and Snake's wiles would never be proof against the beaten owner's sneering disappointment and the worried trainer's thought that pilot-error and female frailty was probably the problem.

Truth be told, other women jockeys have all too often fitted the standard critique. Sensitive skills, well suited to certain horses, but lacking in firepower when the chips are really down. Watching Krone that hot late summer afternoon at Monmouth, where she has for long enjoyed the support of top trainer John Forbes, showed just why she is the exception.

Of course she must be a joy for a horse to carry in the early part of a race, a little bunch of feathers tucked in behind the mane. The animal must feel he is almost running free. Later in the afternoon a reluctant winner called Frothy gets clear of the field on just those terms.

Yet there is a heavily physical side to race-riding. Go to the starting stalls, or lean against the finishing rail and it will whack you in the face. How does Julie handle that? "Well, she's real strong and real tough," says Angel Cordero, at 47 still one of the greatest jockeys in American history. "But obviously she is light. She has to bargain with the horse to come up with answers."

Out on the track at Monmouth Krone has a filly called Paris Rose in front on the final turn. As two other horses come at her the filly's head goes up in both effort and protest. It's a classic situation the world over. Hit her and she will stop. It has to be mind over matter. The Krone message was as compelling as one of those looks Mrs Thatcher lasers out across the dispatch box. "Do this or I'll handbag you." It was going to be close, but Paris Rose did the bidding.

Afterwards, sitting beside the famous swimming pool where Senor Rujano got his comeuppance, Julie wasn't going to waste words on false modesty. "I think I am a much better rider now than before the accident. I was always trying too hard. Now I am a lot more confident."

She has a white polo shirt above her breeches and you can see the wickedly long scar along her left elbow. Without the helmet, her hair is long and blonde and you appreciate that this is now a highly organised young woman. After the morning work she had driven her red Porsche back to her apartment to prepare a sea-food dish for a TV cooking programme. Next week she is on the high-rating David Letterman chat show. She collects antiques, and with a photographer, Jerry Cascano, has just put in a million-dollar bid for an equestrian property in New Jersey.

Nevertheless, the central obsession remains. "I have dedicated my life to the psychology of the horse," she says uncompromisingly before revealing that one of the things she did in the long months out of the saddle was to track down the half-Arabian pony she first won rosettes with in Eau Clair, Michigan. "She is old now," says Julie. "But she can do about 15 circus tricks. I've been teaching a friend's kid with her. She is only 50 inches high, but can jump 2-9."

Krone does not have any racing background but the very unusualness of her childhood has now clearly worked to her advantage. Her father was an art teacher, her mother the Michigan State equestrian champion. As a troubled teenager, torn between accepting offers to go to the Olympics as a gymnast or to the circus as a trick rider, she was inspired by the trail that the young Steven Cauthen cast across the sky.

"He was my inspiration," Krone says. "I read his story and thought 'If he could overcome all the difficulties, so could I.' And do you know," she adds with a touch of hero-worship, "I still never met him."

Her other guiding stars were Shoemaker—"Because of his size, small like me, and because of his wisdom"—and Angel Cordero. "Because he's Angel. He's buoyant, exciting. You can see everything he's doing on a horse."

But by now her own ability is a trophy she studies with almost detached wonderment. "Last month I went up to Saratoga for the first time back." Her eyes flash vivid with the memory. "I rode a big chestnut who carried his head real low. He was a closer. It was a mile-and-a-half race and one of those things where you turn for home six across the track. I was battling all the way to the eighth pole. He finally shook the horses off and began to pull away and another one came at him. It always helps if a horse is game. And he was very game. He kept digging in every time the other came at him. He ran right on and it was tremendous."

There is almost awe in her voice and she becomes very direct. "I am not bragging, because I don't brag, but when I looked at that race afterwards I thought, man I was so good on that horse, so pretty. When things like that happen it gives you confidence to know that you can compete, that maybe you are just a natural. It's just comin' out."

She is called for another race. A midget, almost frail figure that makes you remember Cordero's one proviso. "It will be really big provided she don't get hurt."

The best years of a jockey's life are the thirties. At 27 Julie Krone is heading for immortality. "If I were to win the Kentucky Derby," she had said, "I'll be the most famous person on earth."

The racing passport will open doors in any land where the disease is endemic. The places and the people that will welcome you cover the spectrum and reach far beyond the old-fashioned image of the "sport of Kings". Sometimes the privilege is almost mind-numbing. Like this trip in 1990, a year of destiny if ever there was one.

Mandela's man heads for the winning post
September 23rd 1990

It was a big, burgundy red BMW 735 with a gold, galloping horse mascot on the bonnet. Anywhere in the world that means an owner's car. Even, would you believe it, in Soweto.

Maponya's Motors is a gleaming new BP garage in the Orlando East part of South Africa's sadly troubled black township. Last week the smoke from a million chimneys was, as ever, drifting across the horizon but if you looked over the litter-strewn waste ground you could see the white walls of Nelson Mandela's villa in Orlando West. That's when you remembered where we have all seen that car before.

For it was Richard Maponya who was at the airport when Mandela finally returned to Johannesburg in February. How many noticed that the car which whisked him into the night had a jockey mascot in the colours of the ANC?

The story of South Africa's leading black racehorse owner holds a mirror to some of the frustrations, contradictions and, despite everything, the optimism that pervades a lot of that land today. Mr Maponya, aged 62, has had to overcome all sorts of obstacles and prejudice to establish his empire of supermarkets, garages and bottling plants, and all the while he has made no secret of his support for the lawyer who won him his first trading licence some 30 years ago.

Richard Maponya leads in a winner to show that in South African racing at least you cannot keep a good man down

"Everyone knew I was a friend of Dr Mandela and the ANC," Mr Maponya says. "But I had quite a high profile and it would have created a lot of problems if the authorities had picked me up." Mr Maponya is a big man. He is carefully spoken, impeccably dressed and laughs a lot. Especially he laughs when he thinks about racing.

"It was Mandela and Tambo who challenged the licensing people for me," he says. "But they were 'unavailable' when I wanted to become an owner some 15 years ago. The racing authorities began by putting up all sorts of excuses. They wanted to see my balance sheet, tax returns, everything. But I just would not take no for an answer." Maponya then set about getting the last laugh. Imagine the consternation among the right-wingers when they saw that his first two horses (he now has 16 in training as well as six brood mares at his stud in The Cape) were called Another Color and Black Charger, and that the Maponya black, green and yellow striped colours were the livery of the ANC.

"Some of the jockeys got upset," he says, "because when they went past the stand for the blacks everyone started chanting 'ANC, ANC'. Some jocks said they would never try on one of my horses. But the stewards were fantastic (the legendary Harry Oppenheimer had been his first guarantor). A leading jockey, Jeff Lloyd, said he would ride Another Color and then they won at Newmarket (south-east of Johannesburg) and the whole course nearly came down with the cheering."

With that background you might well imagine an element of comeuppance in Richard Maponya's attitude and indeed in that of the thousands of blacks who now move freely in all racing enclosures. "We have had no unhappy experiences with white people in racing," Mr Maponya says. "Everyone is interested in getting winners, sharing a racecard and talking horses." If those words were spoken by some nodding old blimp, everyone would chide, "He would say that, wouldn't he". But Maponya is a pragmatist and so too are most of the people who run South Africa's magnificently well-appointed racetracks.

The facilities and the atmosphere at Johannesburg's Turfontein course—where on a Saturday afternoon 15,000 people, predominantly black, and many of them from Soweto, pack the stands—put British courses to shame. This is largely because the tracks take up to 5 per cent from both the tote betting pools and from bookmakers who are allowed in limited numbers both on and off the track. But it was also a tribute to what properly run racing can do as a leisure activity. This was a much better example of people being "equal above and below the turf" than you normally see over here.

Of course there are some things that don't seem to square. Old Calvinist hang-ups prevent not only Sunday racing but also stop anyone under 18 entering a racetrack. A country desperate for good foreign bloodlines puts a 40 per cent duty on imported stock. And while much trouble has been taken with the renowned Jockeys Academy at the Summerveld training centre in Natal, no teaching is given to stable lads, and consequently many of the 1,100 horses show the awkwardness of ignorance at the end of the reins.

It was also at Summerveld that racing was last year given a taste of the tribal nightmare—local Zulus and working Xhosa stable lads fighting a running battle which left a dozen dead.

Such stories and other more horrific ones in the wider South African context make the doubts flood in. But back in Soweto Mr Maponya sits and smiles and talks of how much has happened since he first journeyed in from Petersburg to try to get a job as a teacher 45 years ago.

He also nurtures his racing dream. Some years back he bought a horse called Fine Romance which had raced in the royal colours. When its full brother Insular won a big race, Mr Maponya wrote to Buckingham Palace who sent a courteous note in reply.

Soweto must at the moment be about the most difficult place in the world to keep your cool. Richard Maponya is in the centre of it but at times he has an almost regal charm. "If we can put these problems to sleep and move forward together," he says, "then one day there will be a royal visit. She will be sure to come to the racecourse. I will meet the Queen."

At the time of writing the royal meeting has yet to materialise. When it happens have no doubt that the pleasure will be mutual.

Let's close this chapter with a queen and her off-spring. Jenny Pitman visiting her son Mark the day after they had been through an almost ludicrous version of Kipling's "twin impostors" in March of 1991. Racing may be a small world, but at moments like this it's also a special one.

Pain and champagne at a family gathering
March 17th 1991

At first sight, in both triumph and disaster, the mother overshadowed the son. Even in his Cheltenham hospital room on Friday, you couldn't forget that Mark Pitman has a heck of an act to follow.

For mother Jenny sat at the bedside, her bonny face lit up with maternal relief and professional pride. As Mark shifted uncomfortably to ease the ache from his fractured pelvis, he suddenly looked just a pyjamaed boy again. His mother was doing the talking.

She told of how the previous day Mark had driven the once-crippled Garrison Savannah up the crowd-bellowed bedlam of the Cheltenham hill to land the Gold Cup by a whisker. Of how three races later young Pitman took a sickening crash at the second last hurdle and the blue lamp was soon flashing as the ambulance rushed him to Cheltenham General.

Jenny had been worried desperate. A horse had kicked him slap on the spine, it was the sort of fall that could paralyse. Now she could joke about it. "Mark was groaning away in the ambulance," she said, "but he wouldn't let them give him the oxygen. 'Come on,' I said, 'that's just what they gave me when you were being born.'"

She didn't mean to hog the spotlight, she just naturally comes centre stage. It was eight years ago that she won the Grand National with Corbiere, a season later that Burrough Hill Lad also took the Gold Cup at Cheltenham. Jenny Pitman has long since gone into legend as the ultimate intuitive, sometimes irascible ("Do you want to start World War Three?") diva of the National Hunt scene. But Mark?

There was always going to be a no-win deal for the mother's son. If he won races, he was just being loaded on to certainties. If he lost, the critics would say that no other trainer would put up with him.

To some extent that last remark is almost true. Of the 122 rides Mark has had this season, all bar seven have been for Jenny's stable. Every one of his 23 winners have come from that same quarter. For M Pitman race-riding is strictly a family affair.

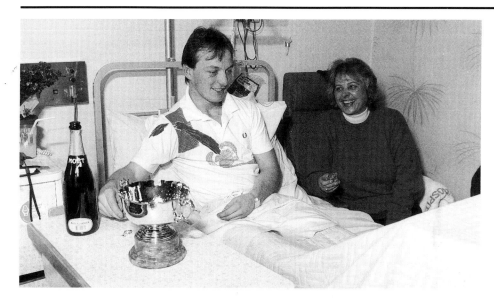

Mother and Son. Jenny and Mark Pitman celebrate the day after they won the Cheltenham Gold Cup with Garrison Savannah, only for Mark to end up in hospital from a later fall (Tony Edenden)

But it has not been feather-bedded. When he broke his collarbone last season it was the ninth occasion that his clavicle had fractured. When he stood on the dais on Thursday he had asked his mother, "Do I have to ride that one in the last?" Even in the full flood of triumph motherhood took a quick shift back for business and for the next 40 minutes Mark steamed off an unwanted pound in the sauna.

Then last year, his first, at 23, as stable jockey, he and Toby Tobias jumped the last in front in the Gold Cup only to be run out of it on the hill by the old Welsh milk horse Norton's Coin. As weariness clutched at Garrison Savannah on Thursday, all that came back and much more.

For it was 18 years to the day that Mark's father Richard Pitman had the Gold Cup snatched from him by The Dikler on the run-in, and then four weeks later he had to endure even sharper heartache when the Grand National eluded him as the exhausted Crisp gave way to the charging Red Rum in the dying strides at Aintree.

All that flashed through Mark's mind as he hurled Garrison Savannah at Cheltenham's final fence. "I had to go for everything," he said, looking across the hospital room on Friday. He knew that failure would have buried him. But he hadn't failed and his smile told you so.

There was a knock on the door. It was Garrison Savannah's owners, carrying a small cardboard box. They unfolded it to reveal the Gold Cup itself, the Holy Grail of steeplechasing.

Mark took it in his hands. They filled it with champagne. Very deliberately he drank from it first. Then he passed it to his mother. For once she didn't say anything but one of the owners did. "I tell you what, son," he said, "you gave that horse one hell of a ride."

2. The Days that Never Fade

Believe it or not, the biggest enemy is boredom. Those who spend their professional life watching races face the occupational hazard of thinking they have seen it all before. That may be a shameful confession, but at least it means that the memories that last are made of sterling stuff.

We start with a classic performance which truly lived up to its name. Rushing from the TV shift to word processor can often garble the judgement. Not this time. Not about El Gran Senor.

El Gran Senor the noblest of them all
May 6th 1984

If you don't like superlatives, this ain't for you. El Gran Senor won yesterday's Two Thousand Guineas with a display of class and power unequalled in modern times.

To say this just one week after hailing last weekend's Whitbread Gold Cup as "the greatest race we have ever seen" might sound as if the pen has been dipped in advertising ink. But El Gran Senor was class, he was speed and above all else this Two Thousand Guineas was as complete an examination as any thoroughbred has had to face since old Charles II first started the whole process up on this same Newmarket Heath 300 years ago.

Not only El Gran Senor, but Lear Fan and Keen brought unbeaten records to the Rowley Mile. Rainbow Quest had some heavy supporters, and Chief Singer had been catching several pigeons on the local gallops. The pace was predictably furious (the winner clocked 1 mile in 37.4sec, almost a second faster than the standard time and 0.72sec quicker than Thursday's One Thousand Guineas) and El Gran Senor's final victory, over Chief Singer, Lear Fan, Rainbow Quest and Keen by two-and-a-half lengths, four lengths, three and three, was absolutely complete.

El Gran Senor finally started 15-8 favourite, but by the time all nine runners were installed (Lear Fan with commendable ease), the expectation that something big might be on hand could be felt right through the huge crowd which thronged the Heath. Sure enough, Lear Fan could only be restrained behind the fast-starting Native Charmer for 100 yards before Brian Rouse found himself towed to the front, and Lear Fan, his tongue hanging way out to the left, took this first colts' Classic of the season by the throat.

Overleaf: 1991 Grand National. The winner, Seagram, second from the right (Chris Smith)

It may all be over in a couple of minutes, but for the duration of the race time seems to expand like a racing driver's mind, and as Lear Fan stormed homeward we looked back and across at those who pursued him. Rainbow Quest was going easily enough, his suspect brakes well suited by the speed

The Maestro and the Masterpiece. Vincent O'Brien with El Gran Senor at Ballydoyle in Tipperary (Chris Smith)

of the gallop. On the outside, Lester Piggott was poised handily enough to overcome Keen's lack of experience, and as the others began to punch and stretch to keep in the race, you could see Chief Singer still moving sweetly at the back, Ray Cochrane husbanding every ounce of his doubtful stamina.

Three furlongs out, and those who had believed that Lear Fan would be able to destroy his field were already worried as Rouse asked him to hit top gear, and behind him Eddery had not moved his hands on El Gran Senor. Two furlongs to go, and Lear Fan had killed most of them, but Eddery still had powder to burn. He moved El Gran Senor to challenge. We thought the race was easily his until we spotted Chief Singer on the rails with Cochrane almost motionless too.

There is a beautiful moment in this sort of race when a jockey has finally to play his hand, and all the pre-race talk gets truly tested. This was Eddery's moment. El Gran Senor answered, and took Lear Fan in a dozen strides, but Cochrane on Chief Singer matched his move. Eddery had to ask again to get an answer which many will believe proves El Gran Senor seriously close to the best thoroughbred ever foaled.

For while it's true that all horses go fast past trees, yesterday's defeated opponents were a long way from being wooden. Of course there is always an element of pre-race hyping, but going round all of the big five early yesterday morning made you think that win or lose this had to be a vintage crop.

Over at the racecourse stables, Lear Fan, Rainbow Quest and El Gran Senor were all out walking. Lear Fan looked massively powerful, Rainbow Quest smaller but classily elegant and El Gran Senor a perfectly made and easy-going professional.

Over at Henry Cecil's Warren Place stables Keen, a fine, masculine-looking chestnut, was out walking; stronger and more handsome than his brother Diesis, who was a brave but sore-footed favourite in last year's race. Cecil's yard is used to the big time, but down in the middle of town Ron Sheather has only been in charge for a couple of seasons. And he's been through most of the mangle that racing demands when times are hard. Chief Singer looked tall and black and brilliant, and the nicest thing about the race was the way he repaid Sheather's faith. In years to come it will be quite something to have been second in El Gran Senor's Guineas.

Twelve months ago, O'Brien and Eddery were successful with Lomond in the same green-and-blue Sangster silks, but now the thoughts go back even further, to Sir Ivor and Nijinsky, O'Brien's other two winners, both of whom went on to take the Derby. Even if the trainer is reluctant to commit himself, you can't get more than 5-2 for the great Epsom Classic, and there was a smile about O'Brien's lips which suggested that this time Vincent really had the one.

Everything that happened afterwards confirmed what the eye had supposed. This was one of the finest performances ever seen on the Rowley Mile. El Gran Senor now lives on through his children but although he ended up winning the Irish Derby he will still be best remembered not for that, or even for the brilliance of the Two Thousand Guineas, but for the race that got away, the tactical disaster of his Derby defeat at Epsom by Secreto.

Lester Piggott has had his memorable defeats, too,

*but in September 1984 he was reminding us that big
races are his craving. Moments like this come only
from a maestro.*

One more prize for the Classics master
September 16th 1984

All the way back to the winner's circle, those famous features remained as
frozen as the Arctic tundra. Then suddenly, after he had dismounted, given
Commanche Run one of those grateful, congratulatory pats, he allowed the
sunshine to flood across his face. Lester Piggott had won the St Leger and
broken the all-time Classic winning record.

It was the living legend's eighth St Leger, and his 28th English Classic,
along a road which began way back in 1954 when, as a pudgy-faced 18-year-
old who thought he would end up as a jump jockey, he won the Derby on
a horse with the supremely appropriate name of Never Say Die.

Indeed, it was very much the implacable side of Piggott's nature that was
needed to achieve this historic success. Commanche Run had taken over
from Alphabatim's pacemaker, Librate, four-and-a-half furlongs from
home, and he then had to fight a long, protracted duel up the Doncaster
straight with Baynoun and Steve Cauthen.

A furlong from home, Cauthen pulled out all the stops, and it looked as
if Piggott would be denied the elusive record he had equalled by winning
the Oaks, last June, and which Frank Buckle had set in those bewhiskered,
less competitive days in the last century.

Yet the story had to be told, and the whole circumstance surrounding
the occasion was a perfect example of the Piggott syndrome at work. There
had been controversy. Remember Commanche Run's owner, the top Singapore trainer, Ivan Allen, had insisted that Piggott rode the horse in place
of the stable jockey, Darrel McHargue. There had been tension.

Trainer Luca Cumani struggled to get Commanche Run into shape after
the horse damaged his knees on Wednesday morning. And then there was
the drama of the race itself.

For a few awkward moments beforehand, Commanche Run seemed
unsure of his lines. He arrived in the paddock looking on the verge of a
nervous breakdown, but the presence of Piggott on his back calmed things
down, and although he then broke from the stalls more freely than Lester
had planned, those strong, sinewy fingers soon transmitted their controlling
message as the pair settled down in second place behind Librate.

Yet in that last desperate furlong another, more compulsive, message
needed to be sent. If one part of Piggott's talent has always been his unique
insight into the mind of the racing thoroughbred, the other side is his raw,
freakish will to win.

It's not always a pretty sight—that pipe-cleaner 5ft 6in frame, and those ultra-short stirrups, let alone his damaged right knee, hardly make for streamlined finishing drives, and as Cauthen and Baynoun got to within a neck, you felt that the young American and his muscular, pumping effort would win the day.

By now Lester was having to dig deep into reserves not normally available to a 48-year-old fresh back from an accident that would have finished most people half his age. The loop of the rein flapped wildly as his left hand stretched out with the horse's neck, the right arm slashed the whip's final demands. At moments like this you can actually see determination as a tangible thing. Commanche Run was the only winner allowed.

The official verdict was a neck, Alphabatim ran on to be a length and a half away third, his stable companion Crazy was fourth, and Shergar's half-brother, Shernazar, an honourable fifth at the end of a mile-and-threequarters, clocked in 3min 9.93sec, very fast indeed considering the rain-softened turf.

It was a first English Classic for the 33-year-old Italian-born but Newmarket-based Cumani. It certainly won't be his last. But as Piggott was muttering afterwards about "just one more year", the 1984 St Leger could well be the maestro's final bow at this level.

Records are made to be broken, and the future will no doubt produce great riders and fine champions, but for those of us who have lived through his era there will never be anything to touch the extraordinary grey-faced centaur that is Lester Piggott.

Piggott will always cast the longest shadow whenever people talk about racing. Not just for his achievements but because of the length and depth of his connections. Piggott was bred and raised for the saddle. He has champion jockeys all through his pedigree. With him you can use big words like "destiny" and "fulfilment".

But then if you dig, there are rich delights in every triumph. Remember this, one March day in 1985.

Forgivable pride and unforgettable joy
March 17th 1985

You could feel the pride at fifty paces. Half a mile from the Cheltenham unsaddling enclosure, and an hour after the victory cheers had died away, Jimmy Fitzgerald patted his Gold Cup winner on the neck. Happiness was having a horse called Forgive 'n Forget.

We were to the back by the horse boxes, and the first of the weary army of punters were beating their retreat after three days of the most jaggedly unexpected results in Cheltenham history. Without his white sheepskin noseband and Mark Dwyer's yellow jockey silks, Forgive 'n Forget looked like just another runner ready for the long trek home. But the closer you got the more you realised that this muscly, bold-eyed chestnut and the smiling windswept man at his head had shared in a triumph so symmetrical that you could almost run your hands around it.

First the much publicised coincidences. Exactly a year ago Forgive 'n Forget and Fitzgerald had started the five-hour drive back to Malton licking the wounds of a gamble that came unstuck. John Francome had been in the saddle for the Sun Alliance Chase but the pairing got so far behind at half-way that the trainer still finds it hard to follow the message in his horse's name.

Only at the beginning of the week it looked as if this year's gamble (struck at 33-1 in the disgruntled aftermath of that other defeat) might not even see the races. While the papers screamed about the problems of Burrough Hill Lad's knee, the Fitzgerald team were prodding and peering at Forgive 'n Forget's foot. And while the favourite couldn't overcome his ailment, Forgive 'n Forget turned the corner albeit shod in "Dot and carry three" style—light aluminium racing plates on three feet with a heavier, steel exercise shoe still on the off fore for fear of reactivating whatever corn or bunion had started the scare.

Then there was a full circle of luck for young Mark Dwyer, whose patience paid off in one of the most competitive and fastest run Gold Cups of recent years. At the last fence seven horses still had a chance, but Mark had saved enough to avoid any lapses in Forgive 'n Forget's sometimes casual jumping and to outgun his rivals on the run-in. Not bad for a 22-year-old County Dublin lad who missed last March with a dislocated shoulder and agonisingly put it out again in the finish of his very first race this season.

But the Irish connection has more than Dwyer to it. Indeed, after one of the worst Cheltenhams ever for the raiding party (Antarctic Bay and Boreen Prince were the sole Irish successes of the meeting), it was bitter-sweet consolation to know that for all their present Yorkshire base, Forgive 'n Forget and his team ought to have shamrock in their ears.

Fitzgerald comes from the Tipperary village of Horse and Jockey (where else?). The owner, Tim Kilroe, originally hailed from Roscommon, and Forgive 'n Forget himself was not only foaled in the Emerald Isle but also won his first race at Leopardstown under the auspices of the redoubtable Barney Curley—and so contradicted his previous less-competitive form that his then jockey and trainer had to take a compulsory holiday.

Curley, gambler and now assistant trainer extraordinaire, was something of an unsung hero in Thursday's piece, for it was three years ago this

February that he consoled a disconsolate Fitzgerald and Kilroe on the death of their best-ever horse, Fairy King, at Kempton with the words "I'll find you one even better."

The former monk who also handled the early days of the 1982 Gold Cup winner, Silver Buck, was not around last week but he will have given that slow old smile to think that however many tens of thousands of punts he originally charged, Forgive 'n Forget was cheap at the price.

But in the end we keep coming back to Fitzgerald and the long road he had taken before holding Forgive 'n Forget so proudly at Cheltenham. A top-class riding career—he won the Scottish Grand National and was fourth in the Gold Cup—ended with a calamitous head injury at Doncaster in 1967. And whilst there may be a record 80 horses in Norton Grange now-adays, there was only one other animal under Jimmy's care when Tommy Stack opened the score on Archer in the August Hurdle at Market Rasen in 1969.

There is, not surprisingly, no lack of blarney in the operation, and those purpling cheeks show that the 49-year-old Fitzgerald can carouse with the best. But no one can hack through the racing jungle on that alone, and Jimmy's recent reputation for being able to deliver coups in either the flat or the jumping scene has not been won without hard work.

Never forgotten. The ill-fated Forgive 'n Forget in action with his long-time partner, Mark Dwyer (A. Johnson)

Amid all the tumult and shouting on Thursday, few noticed that Forgive 'n Forget's bit was taped over with a large black foam cover. "After he ran badly at Ayr we found he had dehydrated, so I put this in his mouth and coated it with glycerine to keep him wet," said Jimmy. And when asked why the horse's charming, if rather stuttering, G-g-g-glasgow stable lad is called "Strappy", the trainer explains that each evening the lad takes one end of the horse and he himself takes the other and they "strap" Forgive 'n Forget over like ostlers of yesteryear.

People talk a lot about luck in racing. It's needed all right, but the trick is to be able to ride it like a surfer when it breaks your way. On Thursday, Jimmy Fitzgerald got it right in to the shore.

There is of course a sad irony in Forgive 'n Forget's glory day. Exactly three years later he was killed in that same Cheltenham arena which saw his finest hour. Steeplechasing can be a bitter game.

Flat racing tends to present fewer terminal problems but in the eighties it began to attract top runners more frequently to the transatlantic "away-match". Many have tried but to date no one has equalled what Pebbles achieved this grey afternoon at Aqueduct. I nearly died of cold but the memory still glows.

The starlet who saved the show
November 10th 1985

Maybe it was the richest, most outlandish triumph in our racing history. Maybe little Pebbles has already been hailed as the greatest travelling mare since Black Bess's unfortunate demise on the road to York. But when she got home in the Breeders' Cup Turf in New York last Saturday, it was still the performance rather than the prize that counted. The star was worth her status.

The achievement cannot be underestimated. Without it, there would have been a very real danger of the whole multi-million dollar Breeders' Cup extravaganza becoming just another American media hype. Screaming about the excitement of "a million dollars on the wire" begins to sound a bit hollow unless there is something out there on the track to justify the superlatives.

Last year at Hollywood Park, in California, the inaugural Breeders' Cup day had a sensational send-off. Of the seven events built into the pro-gramme (five on dirt, two on turf), four of the five dirt races produced winners who became national champions, and the fifth and final dirt race, the $3m Breeders' Cup Classic ended with the most sensational bumping race for the line ever filmed. And as for the two turf races, one of them gave us a new American mile record, the other a French-trained long shot, just for spice. It was a hard script to follow.

True, there was plenty of buzz last week. With 42,000, Aqueduct had its best attendance in years. The $8m bet on the track and the $6m off it was a New York State record, just as the overall turnover of $28m was the biggest single day's wagering in North America. But compared with California, the day was grey. Aqueduct, slap on the end of JFK airport, has never been a fun palace, and the races, with one or two exceptions, only confused their championship standings. And, most critically, the first returns showed that the TV ratings, at which so much of this happening is aimed, seemed to be well down on last year.

Worse still, from an international angle, there appeared to be an almost ridiculous home town advantage, even on the turf.

The structure of all American racetracks is that the turf course is always placed inside the dirt track, which is itself tighter than any major European racecourse. So any of our team, greedy for Breeders' Cup dollars, must first accept that there were to be four turns to the mile. That makes it sharp, but if you start extending your fields (on Saturday they even stretched to 14, despite the normal Aqueduct safety limit of 11), who can wonder if Bill Shoemaker reported it "the roughest race" in which he'd ever ridden.

But dollars talk, and if you have 10 million of them available, it concentrates the mind wonderfully. It's no coincidence that Pebbles' victory and the honourable third by her gelded "walker" Come On The Blues on Sunday, came after their trainer Clive Brittain had fired them round tighter turns than any of his counterparts. "I was so sure she would act on the track," said Clive, "that my real worry was keeping her in condition. I flew her over 16 kilos overweight. She left here 436 kilos, and returned 404. Her racing weight is about 420, so I think we got it about right."

Years ago such detailed talk would have been scoffed at by the upper crust of the training profession. But there has been a meritocracy revolution in English horse care in recent years, and besides Brittain's soaring success with Pebbles you only have to spend a day with the likes of Michael Stoute and Luca Cumani (who both had placed horses at the meeting) to know that they are competitors of the highest international standing.

What you also see is that the enormous range of facilities at their disposal in England (miles of undulating turf, sand, and woodchip gallops—whole counties to hack upon) make the route even of a super-American champion trainer like Wayne Lukas pitiful in its on-track, round-the-barn limitations.

There is no doubt in my mind that our trainers have the advantage in conditioning horses. But the richest races at the end of the year are the other side of the Atlantic, so be prepared for a major shift of winter ambition. Patrick "Napoleon" Biancone now has a dirt course at Chantilly to practise on; he himself is taking a team of 15 to chase dollars in California next month. Be assured that the challenge won't be lost on our men: Clive Brittain already talks of next year's $3m Breeders' Cup Classic for Pebbles; Michael Stoute puckers his lips and says, "It's very interesting."

Mind you, there were other less public triumphs. One evening a diminutive member of the Irish team found himself in one of the less salubrious corners of New York confronted by three very husky locals intent on everything up to GBH and beyond. The odds must have been 500-1 against. But Saturday nights in the pubs back home had not been entirely wasted. One beautifully aimed kick to the privates felled the first local, the rest scarpered. The reputation has gone into legend. As with Pebbles, it's the performance that counts.

A week is a long time in racing. Seven days from celebrating Pebbles' triumph in New York, we were in Newcastle. Another city, another code, and a very much darker side of the picture. This was not for the squeamish.

Browne's Gazette dies in jinxed race
November 17th 1985

Sometimes things go so black that you can believe in curses. In a mysterious but appalling public incident at Newcastle yesterday, Browne's Gazette, one of the great stars of the jumping game, was struck down by a heart attack after less than a minute of the Fighting Fifth Hurdle.

It was in this very race two years ago that the brilliant Ekbalco broke his leg at the second last and had to be destroyed. Yesterday's tragedy happened much earlier. The nine-horse field had jumped but one flight when the thunderbolt struck.

Browne's Gazette, a magnificent, tall, bright bay gelding, already favourite yesterday morning for the Champion Hurdle, staggered beneath Dermot Browne, appeared to slip his hind legs and next thing had slid upside down through the outside rails. Suddenly the only moves he would make were those jerky twitches of the dying.

National Hunt racing has always been a hard game and fractures like Ekbalco's and even, very rarely, a heart attack after long and arduous efforts, are a sad seam in the jumping calendar. But nobody can remember an incident of a top class horse, in the absolute peak of condition, being taken out as Browne's Gazette was yesterday.

"Everything was going quite perfect," said 23-year-old Dermot Browne, who had given the horse his own name when his father bought the gelding unbroken at Ballsbridge, Dublin, three years ago—present owner John

Poynton taking over when the horse became established. "He had jumped the first super. He was beautifully relaxed and I remember thinking to myself 'Riding this is the real McCoy.'"

But then in two, three seconds, it was all changed, changed horribly. "One moment I thought he had put his hind legs in a bit of a hole," said the jockey. "Then I thought he had broken something, and tried to get a tug at him. Next, he was careering for the rails and I baled out."

There is something so nakedly shocking about seeing such instant and violent and public a death that it's hard to get a grip on reality. Browne's Gazette started yesterday with 11 victories already to his name. He was trained by the Dickinsons at Harewood. He had the best prospects of any horse in the kingdom.

"I am very sorry for all of them," said Dermot afterwards. "For the owner, for all those who liked the horse." Then, very simply, he added: "I haven't taken it in yet. But losing him is like losing a brother."

In a quite ludicrous coincidence, the one man who best would have known how Browne had felt, was actually to put his own special stamp on the afternoon. Two years ago it had been Jonjo O'Neill who had cradled the stricken Ekbalco's head in his arms. Yesterday he overwhelmed the race's closing stages with a vintage display on the almost over-appropriately named Out Of The Gloom.

You wouldn't have given him much chance as Graham Bradley brought Ballydurrow with a surging run to jump the last flight and go three lengths clear on the flat. But Jonjo knew that Ballydurrow is a one-kick horse and as he regathered Out Of The Gloom to launch a uniquely intuitive and forceful counter-attack there was only going to be one result.

It was not really a pretty sight. Some might even doubt O'Neill's statement afterwards that: "He loves you to get after him." But the fact is that O'Neill's own determination and, let's not dodge it, a few fairly urgent cracks of the whip, inspired Out Of The Gloom to the greatest win of his career.

There were three other meetings yesterday and no performance better than Very Promising's final justification of his name in the H and T Walker Goddess Chase at Ascot. All sorts of things have been wrong with Very Promising and his stable over the last 12 months but from the way he put as good a horse as Buck House adrift those ailments are clearly in the past.

Yet in the end the day will always belong to those last terrible moments when Browne's Gazette went cartwheeling into oblivion. A reminder perhaps to all of us who enjoy the vitality and absurdity of the racing game—that even in the prime of life—we are only on the edge of it.

Sometimes not even a camera can catch the moment.
Go to the races, go in close, and very occasionally you

*will see something that grips you by the throat. Here
are two moves so strong that for me they will never
need the video. Pat Eddery's Arc win on Dancing
Brave, but first Jonjo O'Neill on Dawn Run at
Cheltenham.*

One last great leap into immortality
March 16th 1986

The truth wasn't only in the shouting. The roar that greeted Dawn Run as she
battled back to win at Cheltenham on Thursday would have taken the roof
off the Abbey. But it was only half the story.

What happened afterwards has of course already gone into legend as the
greatest shared rejoicing between horse and rider and race fans that the old
game has ever seen. We have had popular horses and favourite jockeys before
but never has the sun-bursting, arm-aloft moment of triumph been so perfectly caught or so rapturously welcomed as when Jonjo O'Neill punched his
fist in the air and the massive Gold Cup crowd bellowed its response.

The overwhelming current of joy which then brought chaos enough to
flatten every wall in the Cotswolds had a lot to do with the glorious, gallant,
heart-on-sleeve character of Jonjo O'Neill, with Dawn Run's history-
making Gold Cup–Champion Hurdle double, and with singing Irish pride
at the separate fairy-tale achievement of her owner and trainer. But the
crowd rejoiced above all because they had seen, and had sensed, the drama
and difficulties and final lung-busting bravery that had won the mare and
her rider their piece of immortality.

Out away from the enclosures we felt the noise afterwards because we
had heard the silence before. Dawn Run had been the last of the 11 runners
to trot up for that traditional wishful look at the first of the Gold Cup
fences. Atop her was not Jonjo the cheerful cherub but O'Neill the hardened, close-lipped professional. The mare fidgeted while he pulled at his
off-side stirrup leather. You caught a hint of tension as he tilted his chin
upwards before cantering back. A little ripple of heedless chatter ebbed
across from the hospitality tent. A whole hillside held its breath.

Sometimes the Gold Cup's early stages can be a happy, hunting canter
before the real race later on. Not this year, not even at the first. O'Neill
put Dawn Run in front but the others were upsides and travelling. If ever
pressure in sport had a meaning it was in Jonjo's face as he looked at that
fence through Dawn Run's ears. They met it on a long stride. His body
thrust down and forward. The big mare came up and over in one huge
stream of power. One fence gone, 21 to come.

The battle plans were clear already. Run and Skip would harry the mare

Jonjo's joy. Jonjo O'Neill and Dawn Run ride a great wave of happiness back to the Cheltenham winner's circle in 1986 (Chris Smith)

from the start and expose her inexperience. Wayward Lad and Forgive 'n Forget would stalk the pair of them. There was to be no quarter. The track record would be broken.

But the first blood went to the mare. As they streamed away from the stands to the downhill third fence Run and Skip pushed up at a furious gallop only for Dawn Run to throw in a fantastic jump. Run and Skip missed his and almost fell. For a while that gave her a respite and there was a time on that first circuit when you could believe that her class and brilliance might make this into a royal procession.

Well, Princess Anne may have been land-rovering around as a fascinated observer, Dawn Run may have put in another long, low accurate leap as she came past us the second time, but out on the track the pack were still after the queen and soon they would get a bite.

It came at the "water", the lowest and simplest jump on the track, but, with Run and Skip hassling again, Dawn Run lost concentration and dropped her hind legs with such a splash that Graham Bradley's goggles were momentarily blinded with spray aboard Wayward Lad.

So she was vulnerable. The pursuers chased close and four fences later, five from home, they almost had her. For once, O'Neill and the mare got their wires crossed, she hit the fence hard and low and the 34-year-old former champion had to draw on his well of experience to keep her head up and his body down.

"Yes, I thought she was beat then," said Run and Skip's rider Steve Smith Eccles afterwards. "But she hung on and then stayed them out of it."

They were the necessarily laconic words of the seasoned campaigner but they hardly do justice to the absolutely crucial moment as the four principals raced to the second last, right in front of us.

By now all ideas of an easy Dawn Run triumph were long abandoned. Run and Skip was still at her, and Wayward Lad and Forgive 'n Forget had arrived with legs to spare. She wasn't going to win and only a brave, brave, jump would even keep her in the argument.

Subsequent events, gloriously replayed a thousand times, were to show that Wayward Lad and Forgive 'n Forget were to run calamitously out of trumps on the flat having played their cards when the race was between them at the last. But Dawn Run's unforgettable late surge could never have got to them without staying in touch at the second last.

All four horses had been in a line. Dawn Run was getting the worst of it. O'Neill would have to dig deep. In the last three strides he became the tiger. With body, and boots and whip he drove her in and demanded a long, lone one. He got it.

Even more than the incredible crescendo of the finish, that was the moment. It was the most vital, most brilliant jump of Jonjo's life. It was the very heart of sport. It meant that those cheers will last as long as memory holds.

Dawn Run lives on in that day but tragically not in the flesh. A second shot at the French Champion Hurdle brought a heavy fall, and the abattoir.

The thought is enough to put you off the French connection so here is an afternoon when the sun truly shone. From O'Neill at Cheltenham to Eddery at Longchamp. Different disciplines but both of them unique.

Eddery's finish: brave, brilliant, unbelievable
October 13th 1986

As with all masterpieces, the more you study the better it looks. Pat Eddery and Dancing Brave's victory on Sunday was more than a triumph. It was the most brilliant final trump that racing has ever seen.

To understand fully last week's excitement you must wind back to the 800-metre mark and remember that the unique thrill of top class flat racing is that a jockey only has one shot. If he moves too soon he gets run out of it; too late and he never collects.

Eight hundred metres out in this Arc there were still plenty of pilots with power beneath them. Eddery had Dancing Brave back 11th of the 15 runners. He could see Shardari, Darara, Shahrastani and Bering all poised to sprint. He had to be ready.

With the fastest ever Arc finish about to start, did Pat move out to cover Bering's kick? On a horse whose only defeat was when he got impossibly out of position at Epsom, did Eddery close up for the winning burst? Did he hell! He put Dancing Brave back inside and let the race develop. If he lost, the Seine wouldn't be deep enough.

For a moment you couldn't believe your eyes. He was giving the others a start and, spread eight-wide across the track, they flattened quite furiously for the line. These were crack horses and now Dancing Brave had to move across behind them before even beginning his effort. By any ordinary criteria he had got the cards wrong. But this was no normal beast, no ordinary man. And, as with all greatness, what was seen next will never be forgotten.

For about a dozen strides horse and rider went almost desperately to work with little effect on the gap. Then suddenly those sinewy legs bit deep into the Longchamp turf and propelled this gleaming bay wonder towards the others with a momentum which made victory certain long before he knifed past at the death.

He had played last. But he got it right. The trick, the game, the glory was taken.

To do this had needed that astonishing, casual, match-winning cool that makes Eddery one of the greatest instinctive jockeys ever foaled. It also needed a horse with a most extraordinary switch-on of speed, and no praise can be too high for the way that Guy Harwood and his team had brought their colt through seven pressurised big-race months to reach this highest peak on Sunday.

Their training centre down at Pulborough in Sussex has long been a byword for the most modern methods of thoroughbred assessment, everything from video cameras to muscle biopsy, so it's fitting that Longchamp was able to give statistical proof of the visual wonder of Dancing Brave's finish.

The Paris clock showed that the record overall time of 2min 27.7sec for the Arc de Triomphe's 2,400 metres (1½ miles) included a closing quarter of 22.80, from the moment that Shardari passed the 400-metre mark in front to when Dancing Brave crossed the line. As Dancing Brave had at least five lengths to make up in that last section and you allow 0.1 seconds a length, this means that he finished as fast as Europe's top sprinter Double Schwartz in the 1,000-metre (five furlongs) Prix de l'Abbaye an hour before the Arc.

The acute pressure in the straight is further shown by the rare fact that this closing quarter was the fastest stage of the race. Even more exceptional for a mile-and-a-half event, the last 200 metres were as swift as any. 11.40 on the board, little change out of 11 seconds for Dancing Brave. Compare this with Sagace's last quarter of 11.90 and 12.10 in 1985, or Mill Reef's of 12.10 and 12.40 in 1981 and you appreciate that nobody's done it quicker.

Even by Eddery's standards this was a finish to treasure, and for a moment on Sunday he let slip such phrases as "he was terrific, electrifying. When I asked him he really jumped."

But at Ascot on Friday Pat was back to his usual unexaggerating self. "I switched to the inside coming into the straight to avoid taking off from the bend," he said, as if discussing some job in the office. "Then I deliberately

The finest finish. Dancing Brave and Pat Eddery (third from the right) in the midst of their dazzling winning sprint at Longchamp (Chris Smith)

gave them first run because I didn't want to get there too soon. When you come off the bridle it takes a stride or two for him to quicken but when he does it's very fast and I don't think any of the others thought a horse could do what Dancing Brave did to Bering."

It all sounds a bit like yesterday's marketing plan, not the race of the century. But then that's part of the secret.

The memory goes back to just before the start on Sunday. The horses are being loaded, the jockeys frowning in concentration. All except Eddery. He's awake and alert all right but the way he pats his horse and steps into the stall is devoid of tension. He looks like a commuter wanting a good position on the train so he can play cards on the journey.

Give him the pack. On this form he could deal with the Devil.

Dancing Brave became a benchmark of greatness.
Three years later we thought we had found his equal.
Nashwan was clearly exceptional but the
circumstances around him, his crippled trainer
apparently at the wrong end of royal favour, meant
that the emotions got involved.
   Tempers have cooled now but writing this, which I
still believe to be a true reflection of the moment,
almost had me in the Tower.

Nashwan's Two Thousand Guineas
May 7th 1989

The figure in the wheelchair was hunched and pale, but the gleam in the eye as Nashwan rocketed over the line on the big TV screen was unmistakable. For Major Dick Hern, the Two Thousand Guineas was the purest of triumphs.

Racing has a happy knack of creating fables in heroic vein, and by any standards the Dick Hern saga has to go into legend. Crippled in a hunting accident five years ago, the great trainer endured heart surgery last summer, and what amounts to a royal eviction order during the winter. Nashwan's victory was a statement stronger than the harshest of words.

But the race must come first. A Classic race begs the superlative, and history may well show we got it. Nashwan may have got home only by a length and two halves from the determined pursuit of Exbourne, Danehill and Markofdistinction, but in clocking 1min 36.44sec for the mile, he put up the fastest-ever electrically recorded Guineas time and, much more importantly, he left an impression that transcends the racing game.

For in all sport there is nothing to match the big, powerful athlete who is also light on his feet. Nature rarely bestows both gifts, and when she does, you have to be wary that the mind may be weak. So it was that even hardened cynics were being swayed by Nashwan even before the starter gave the order to begin loading the 14 runners into the stalls for this General Accident-sponsored £100,000 prize.

We had all heard of the gallops which had meant the sudden blocking of all phone lines from West Ilsley in the early part of last month. But it's when a horse comes into the crowded paddock, walks out into the buzz of the parade and hacks to the start that you begin physically to assess where your money will be placed. With Nashwan, big, composed but wonderfully light-stepping, the reassurance was magnificent.

In fact, the public participated in the gamble in an unprecedented way that must be unique to Britain. A month ago, this beautifully bred colt was still 40-1 for the Guineas because, strictly on the form book, his two victories last season did not amount to much. But bush-telegraph tales that Nashwan had worked better at home than any horse since Hern's last Two Thousand winner, Brigadier Gerard in 1971, meant that the flood of money went way beyond the stable, and Nashwan went off a 3-1 favourite.

His biggest rival in the market was also supported more on reputation than performance. The Irish colt Saratogan had run third to Nashwan's admirable but lesser-rated stable companion, Prince of Dance, in last year's Dewhurst Stakes, but he came to Newmarket with his trainer Vincent O'Brien saying that he compared favourably with his four previous Guineas winners.

Saratogan eventually finished a sorry ninth, only slightly less disappointing than the Craven Stakes winner, Shaadi, who only beat three home. Walter Swinburn could not explain Shaadi's lapse, which was made particularly painful by the brilliant run of his Craven Stakes victim, Exbourne, who looked as if he might well run Nashwan out of it as the leaders went for the punch up the final hill.

Greensmith had done sterling work as pacemaker for the Abdulla pair, Danehill and Exbourne, but Nashwan had broken freely and was always going to find himself a target when the pacemaker gave way. Two-and-a-half furlongs out, Carson had to commit himself. Exbourne, Danehill and the once-raced Markofdistinction went with him. All of them had their chance, but with sentiment washing all round and into the betting shop where the Hern wheelchair parks itself, Nashwan answered Carson's urgings in decisive fashion.

It was a victory that had Epsom Derby written all over it, and bookmakers were running for cover with a mere 5-2 offered for the next Classic, four weeks away.

Dick Hern has always been wary of the public interview, but he agreed to go on TV. He was the old Dick Hern, paying tribute to the work of all his staff, the talent of his horse and coming back with such comments as: "He could gallop down the side of a house" when asked about Nashwan's ability to act around Epsom's gradients, and finally a challenging: "Who's going to beat him?"

But the one proviso Hern made about the interview was that I should not ask him about the move which, if present plans stand, he will be forced to make at the end of this season.

He is still too loyal to publicly query the decision made by the Queen and her racing manager, Lord Carnarvon, to refuse the 69-year-old trainer an extension of his lease, but it has to be reported that feeling among the racing fraternity is now running at an extraordinary height, one notable urging me "to go for the jugular" in this column.

In the glow of Classic triumph, let's just confine ourselves to a practical point. Nashwan is now the best horse at West Ilsley. And his owner, Sheikh Hamdan, who is fiercely loyal to Hern, is likely to race him as a four-year-old just as he has his half-brother, Unfuwain, who was so impressive at

Happiness was a horse called Nashwan. Willie Carson greets the wheelchair-bound Dick Hern in the Newmarket winner's circle and their looks say it all (Ed Byrne)

Newmarket on Friday. What on earth is the point in forcing Nashwan and his trainer away from the place to which they are bringing glory?

Whatever the original intentions of the Queen's decision, it has now backfired. There is no action in the whole of racing that would now be more popular, or necessary, than a royal change of heart.

Happily Dick Hern's move was delayed a year and as Nashwan was denied his chance to run as a four-year-old the edges were smoothed off a situation which hurt all parties more than any of them could ever have imagined. No one doubts that the road was paved with good intentions but for a time we certainly seemed headed for the bonfire.

Thank heaven racing is a moveable feast. Dick Hern trained the super sprinter Dayjur the next season before moving to a high-tech new base near Lambourn. William Hastings Bass (now Lord Huntingdon) began a dignified stewardship of West Ilsley.

However, most race watching is done not from Newmarket or Ascot—or indeed from any other race track. An abandoned day at Sandown gave an excuse to look at the game through a Betting Shop Punter's eyes. Since SIS started its service in 1986 the "BSP" has become the most action-hit viewer on this earth. On this particular Saturday there was plenty on offer.

Worlds apart but it's still the same old game
February 4th 1990

Bill Shoemaker bowed out at Santa Anita last night, but he is not forgotten; from what we could see of Alex Greaves yesterday, not even at Southwell.

Now, the limited spectator delights of a soggy February Saturday on the Nottinghamshire track's all-weather surface are about as far as you can get from the Californian sunshine and the San Gabriel mountains which were the setting for Shoemaker's long-awaited finale. But there was something about Alex's victory on Irish Passage that would not have disgraced the old Shoe himself.

For wherever you look at it—and we were peering through the SIS screens at the Ladbrokes shop in Esher after Desert Orchid and company were rained off at Sandown—this is still thoroughbred racing, and certain truths are permanent. One of them is a saddle-borne version of Kipling's, "If you can keep your head when all about you . . ." That was one of

Shoemaker's strongest suits, and although Alex, the queen of Southwell, is some 8,800 winners behind the legend, it is already one of hers.

Irish Passage was 6-4 favourite in an 18-horse field for the one-mile claiming race. After a furlong, he had only five behind him, but judging by the angle and stillness of the lady on his back, his pilot was not worried. As the race unwound, that stillness took shape, so that as they came off the turn Irish Passage had enough energy and lung-power in reserve, enabling him never to be in serious trouble in the final duel with Gothic Ford.

To be frank, Alex Greaves is not going to win too many battles in a finish at the moment. She looks a bit weak and uncoordinated in those last dozen punching strides to the post. Finishing power will never be her forte, and the reason she has ridden twice as many winners as her nearest Southwell rival is that she does the Shoemaker thing. "Think of the horse," he always used to say. "Think of how it's running where it wants to be. You don't win many races in the last few jumps."

Alex herself was content to deliver old lines from young shoulders. "I was never worried," she said. "Everything went according to plan."

And, when pressed about the phenomenal run that has taken her from someone no one had heard of to just about the only person (at Southwell, anyway) that anyone ever talks about, she merely added: "The success hasn't sunk in yet."

Irish Passage was Alex's 15th victory, and David Barron the trainer's 15th, too, since fibresand flat racing started in October. The trouble with watching it in a betting shop is you tend to bet such runs will continue. So it was that the winnings were laid on the combination's Captain Brown in something called the Carlton-on-Trent Handicap. You can guess the result.

Other failures riddled an afternoon spent in the sort of place in which more than 90 per cent of all betting money is lost. Exactly whether you are in a sport or a business becomes a bit questionable as the cashier helps you along, but there was a certain seedy, hopeless charm as we pushed through the afternoon.

Two punters had come down from Manchester just to see Desert Orchid. They wished they hadn't after Yukosan got beaten in the first at Southwell. A famous golfer silently ground up his betting slip when Martin Pipe's Bramber never threatened in the second.

There were hopes that fortunes could be restored at Wetherby, but Merano, the hot favourite, was beaten half a mile out in the first, and although Tort duly obliged in the novice chase, the winning dividend was so small it seemed miserly to collect it.

All this time, a disembodied voice invoked us to get involved with other sports, Liverpool v Everton starting at 3p.m., Spurs v Norwich on Sunday,

England and France already under way. Why oh why didn't we take some of that 6-4 England?

But the final turn reverted to Southwell. In the 2.55, Dean McKeown, the ace northern jockey who had begun his winter in India, was loaded up on the day's absolute banker, a four-year-old called Trip To The Moon.

For one mile of the 11-furlong journey, the long McKeown back was tilted confidently low on the favourite. Some justice would surely be done. But then his elbows began to move, the confidence collapsed like a punctured tyre and a 33-1 no-hoper called Hopea sailed up the outside to victory. Frantic calls were put through to Southwell to get this nonsense explained.

After all, Hopea had not run for six months, and her last recorded public appearance was to be knocked down at the Newmarket December Sales for 2,200 guineas, less than you would pay for a show pony.

She had, in fact, been bought as a hack for the wife of David Thom, her new trainer. He first came to fame some 30 years ago with fine horses like Mig and Prince Hansel and had, as I remember it, some connection with a herd of cows.

It was not recorded whether Hopea was on to milkshakes every night, but her new role as a hack clearly suited her. Mrs Thom began to report more and more power under the bonnet and racing was once again put on the schedule. The rest is history.

If Southwell is one of racing's "reps", Aintree remains the greatest stage of all, and the Grand National report on the Saturday night is the biggest single hassle for the racing hack—a thousand hectically typed words through the keyboard to an audience who, thanks to TV, probably know a lot more about what happened in the race than you do.

In 1990 it was also my first piece for the Independent on Sunday *after 15 years with the* Sunday Times. *It's a good job I knew something about the winner.*

Dreams come true for Mr Frisk
April 8th 1990

All the joy and all the sadness. Marcus Armytage, a 25-year-old racing journalist, lived out the amateur's dream with a record-breaking ride on Mr Frisk to win yesterday's Grand National. But at the end two horses, Roll-A-Joint and Hungary Hur, lay dead and the Aintree arguments rage on.

Roll-A-Joint, who won seven races last season, broke his neck at the

Canal Turn and died instantly. Hungary Hur, the highest rated Irish hope, broke his leg on the flat before the 18th and had to be destroyed. Roll-A-Joint's jockey, Simon McNeill, came back a shattered man; but is it a sin to think the National risk, indeed all jump-racing risks, worth taking?

Marcus Armytage never had any doubts, even before yesterday's ride of a lifetime. Both his parents are trainers; his mother, Sue, was an international show-jumper; and from toddler's togs his second home was in the saddle. But many a horsey home has boys like that. They don't usually end up dazzling the world in the Grand National. But then they don't often team up with a talent like Mr Frisk.

Man and horse, and might-have-been: that's always the story as we put the pieces of the race together. Marcus Armytage, a laid-back achiever who this week enters the most hectic part of his writing season as Newmarket correspondent of *The Racing Post*. Mr Frisk, a frenetic worrier who has been calmed by the feminine touch of his trainer's wife, Tracy. And Uncle Merlin, the American horse who was cruising beside Mr Frisk when he stumbled and dislodged Hywel Davies at Becher's Brook second time round.

That awful, saddle-screwing, arm-wrenching moment will haunt Hwyel until they put him in the coffin, and was the most crucial event in all 8 minutes 47.8 seconds of this first sub 9-minute National, 13 seconds under Red Rum's record 1973 time.

The tempo of the race was dictated by the Uncle Merlin–Mr Frisk tandem. Rinus, Sir Jest, the favourite Brown Windsor and the eventual second Durham Edition began to emerge as the leading pursuers, but it was these two who set the pace, who caught the eye. Truth be told, it was Uncle Merlin who was the more impressive. Magnificently though Mr Frisk was jumping for Marcus (his perfectionist mother only logged one rider-mistake), Uncle Merlin was quite brilliant. Last year he had won America's biggest prize, the Maryland Hunt Cup, over unforgiving solid timber. In less than half a dozen runs in England's soggy winter, he has looked just an ordinary horse. Back to the lightning-fast ground he loves, he took the Aintree challenge as an inspiration.

Indeed, to watch the two leaders jumping down to Becher's on the second circuit was to understand why, for all its faults, the National makes addicts of us. Bold horses, brave men, reaching for fences and soaring clear, right down to the famous fence they came. Uncle Merlin's stride brought him a little close, Davies aimed him a fraction left to help with take off. It got Uncle Merlin up well, but he came down fairly steep and as the impact of the drop bit on his forelegs, the American horse scrabbled with his feet and stumbled out with his neck. It is a standard mistake, even at this successfully remodelled Becher's. Ninety-nine times out of a hundred it would have

Mr Frisk and Marcus Armytage jumping high, wide and handsome at Liverpool in 1990 (George Selwyn)

merely given Davies a wrench. But this time the hundred came up. As Hywel's long, lean frame clamped down on to the saddle to right the balance, Uncle Merlin's back arched up sharply, threw his partner forward and, as the horse moved sideways to correct his weight, the man's instant death-grip on the rein was not enough. Hwyel Davies won the National five years ago on Last Suspect, but yesterday will be etched just as deep.

For now the young man's dream was suddenly slammed in Marcus Armytage's face. Out clear in the National, a strong horse beneath you, eight fences to jump, no reason to stop.

"To be honest," he said afterwards, "my first thought was that he might refuse at the next once he found himself on his own. He got over that and then I kept trying to keep him relaxed and hold him together."

They are simple words, but they adorn what will remain one of the finest jumping performances ever seen at Liverpool. As Mr Frisk set for home from the Canal Turn, the hounds were closing in the chase. Rinus, Sir Jest, Brown Windsor and in particular Durham Edition had the leader in their sights.

It is the stage at which one mistake gives the initiative back to the pursuers. Television has now given us incomparable close-ups of how the mistakes never came, of how again and again Marcus saw a stride, threw his heart far out over and drew a magnificent morale-lifting leap from his partner.

Nevertheless the final play was still to come. Durham Edition and Chris Grant know Aintree: both have known the heartbreak of second place. They had to challenge late, and going to the last they were within reach.

The final battle. Marcus Armytage and Mr Frisk grit their teeth as Durham Edition and Chris Grant (partly hidden) chase them up the long Aintree run in (Alec Russell)

Another wonderful, soaring jump from Mr Frisk—but now Durham Edition was closing. Four hundred and fifty yards of the run-in were left.

As they met the "elbow", Grant threw everything at Durham Edition. Marcus turned his whip over and thumped Mr Frisk hard. For an awful moment he lost his rhythm as he hit again. Everything could be lost. But Grant had nothing left while Armytage now recalled his father's advice that morning. "He told me I was sure to be tired, not to go for the whip," Marcus said. "So I just tried to balance Mr Frisk for those last few yards, and he was always holding the other horse."

A year ago in my other hat with *The Racing Post*, I was trying to persuade a promising but slightly unconvinced young journalist that the best thing for his future was to get his A levels in flat racing by becoming the Newmarket correspondent. "But I would like to go on riding," he said. "There's the chance that I could ride Mr Frisk in the Grand National." Plenty of bullying was needed, and assurances given that of course we would like him to ride at Aintree. Now he has.

Marcus followed that by writing a brilliant account of this ride of rides under the blunt but accurate banner headline "How I Won the Grand National".

He said afterwards that he found the writing almost more arduous than the race itself. My jockey days are almost too long ago to remember, but writing dramas are all too close at hand. Like this one after the Oaks at Epsom in 1990.

We had a deadline so close up to Channel 4's TV programme that I had to sneak in the story paragraph by paragraph whenever the cameras were off me. Ten minutes before the end of the show I opened the word processor once again only for one of the computer chips to default and the whole story to vanish before my eyes. This happens to all of us hacks from time to time but it's almost like the death of a loved one. Certainly it put this scribbler into desperate straits. With the clock ticking the only resort was to rush to the car and ad lib over the mobile phone.

Thank heaven Salsabil was a strong enough story to let us just about get away with it.

Salsabil's extra gear is decisive
June 10th 1990

Salsabil did not just win yesterday's Oaks. She sent out a challenge as old as the Wicked Queen's in *Snow White*. Is she the fairest of them all?

And not just of her own sex either. For the way she drew five long lengths clear of Game Plan and Knight's Baroness was even more impressive than Quest For Fame's Derby victory on Wednesday. And although her time of 2min 38.7sec was more than a second slower than the Derby, this was much softer ground and so in terms of merit was probably superior.

Willie Carson, riding his fourth winner of the Oaks and 50th of the season, summed it up beautifully afterwards. "She handled everything well because she's got class. If you have class you can always position yourself easily because of an extra gear. She's very good but she surprised me how well she got home."

What this all means, of course, is that the much-awaited showdown between Salsabil and In The Groove never materialised. Indeed, the other heavily fancied runner, Kartajana, also failed to fire and was struggling at the top of the hill, and finished last.

To be fair, In The Groove threatened for a long time to unleash the brilliant speed which won her the Irish One Thousand Guineas, but when Cash Asmussen moved through to close on the leaders in the straight he was very soon fighting a hopeless cause.

Meanwhile, up in front, the suitably named Ahead was disputing things with Pat Eddery's ride Cameo Performance, followed by Knight's Baroness with Carson poised on the rails just behind them. Down through Tattenham Corner they came with In The Groove still stalking them, but the real action was to happen up front.

It is crucial to remember that after Salsabil had won the One Thousand Guineas at Newmarket her trainer, John Dunlop, was clearly doubtful whether she would last the extra half-mile. For Carson too the new trip was, in his own words, unknown territory, so what happened in the half-dozen seconds when the horses straightened up with three furlongs to run was a classic dilemma of the jockey's role.

For although Carson still had plenty of power running beneath him, his passage out right was being blocked by Richard Quinn on Knight's Baroness, riding so hard that he was to earn himself a three-day suspension for excessive use of the whip. As Carson manoeuvred round behind Knight's Baroness, the way clear began to be closed by the South African jockey Basil Marcus on the outsider Game Plan. A moment's hesitation and that door too would be slammed shut.

Doubts of stamina or not, Willie Carson has not ridden 3,000 winners and 16 Classics since he was the smallest paperboy in Stirling by being

On their own. Willie Carson and Salsabil power home at Epsom in the 1990 Oaks (Ed Byrne)

riddled with indecision. Through the gap he went, Salsabil accelerated clear and the unknown territory had arrived.

"I really came too soon," Willie said with that famous cackling laugh afterwards, "but I didn't want to mess about and she kept on galloping really well. Mind you, I wasn't exactly looking around for the others."

Provided a horse does not pull desperately hard, such a commonsense approach to the problem of getting the distance is usually infinitely preferable to dropping way out at the back of the field with the chance of being trapped into the hopeless position made so unhappily famous by Dancing Brave four years ago. The question now is whether Salsabil will meet Quest For Fame and the other colts in a head-to-head to dispute the championship honours. Whatever the outcome, a blue-blooded visit to Nashwan on her retirement to the paddocks seems certain.

In the press conference afterwards, Salsabil's owner Sheikh Hamdan Al Maktoum claimed that his big ambition was not so much the Arc but a crack at the colts in the Champion Stakes, sponsored of course by his own country of Dubai.

Either way, there can be some rejoicing at the end of his Derby week that some genuine stars have emerged from what had seemed a decidedly murky season. Quest For Fame is improving very fast and on Derby Day was an impressive winner by any standards.

Most extraordinary of all has been the fairy-tale start to the training career of Roger Charlton, who was saddling Quest For Fame just three days after he had tightened the surcingle on Sanglamore before that colt won the French Derby.

Yet just three months ago, 41-year-old Charlton was anxiously winding up the string he had inherited from Jeremy Tree at Beckhampton with a view to winning some races early in the season. The best he could hope for was from "a couple of nice maidens" that were to be Quest For Fame and Sanglamore. Mind you, like a deputy taking on the headmastership of a great school, he was succeeding to one of the finest training centres in the land and following a great man in Jeremy Tree.

Although Beckhampton has seen a dozen Derby winners return beneath the trees, none of them unfortunately were trained during the Tree era. Nonetheless, the courtesy and candour which were the hallmark of his tutor have clearly rubbed off on Charlton. Through all the media hassle, he kept a cool head and a patient tongue, something which has not always applied to his fellow trainers recently.

Last month, one mighty member of the profession was asked some innocuous question by one of us hacks and suddenly flipped his lid, narrowed his eyes and said "If you ask me anything else, I'll kick you in the balls."

Perhaps race-riding is the safest game.

Salsabil had quite a year before she blew out in the Arc. There was something about 1990 that was always heading for a showdown. On the last Saturday in October we got it.

History overshadowed by a death in the afternoon
November 4th 1990

There never was and there never will be a racing day to match it. At the end we had supped overfull—of glory, but of horrors too.

For as the images tumble through of that extraordinary Breeders' Cup Saturday at Belmont last week, one moment always finally spins up to the top. Not the astonishing shadow-jump that robbed Dayjur of the most brilliant speed achievement in the sport's history, nor even the eerily wonderful moment when you realised that Piggott's comeback had topped everything that even he had done. No, the memory we have to live with is of death at the racetrack. Even in murder-hardened New York, a horse could make them cry.

Of course equine tragedies are endemic to the racing game, and not just when there are the crashing risks of such obstacles as Becher's Brook. The worst accident of Willie Carson's career came when the filly Silken Knot snapped both legs early in the straight at York in 1981. But last week's death of Go For Wand was as bad as you could ever see.

For she was billed as the ultimate star on the biggest stage American racing has to offer. The very point of the seven-race, $10m Breeders' Cup Day when it was founded in 1984 was to draw the spotlight. They sure had succeeded this year, with 50,000 people at Belmont and four and a half hours of live networked television.

The cards were printed, the seats were sold, and for the Americans the most eagerly awaited event of all was the promised duel between the three-year-old Go For Wand and the six-year-old Bayakoa in the Breeders' Cup Distaff, a race that would decide who was "Queen of the Breed".

There we go, hoisting horses with human characteristics. That was half the problem with the disaster that disfigured last Saturday. Go For Wand was "the young queen", last year's top two-year-old, and only twice beaten in 12 starts.

The Argentinian Bayakoa was "the old queen", winner of this race last year and of 20 of her 35 races. The local papers had lots of phrases like "When the two ladies race head-to-head something will have to give." No one thought it would be Go For Wand herself.

What made it worse was that this was the third of the Breeders' Cup races and the senses were already under siege. We had begun with the sprint, Dayjur's race, it took just 70 seconds to complete but there was so much incident from stalls to wire, that it took us about three replays to work out what had happened.

This was the race the British team had been most tense about—hoping against hope that Dayjur's speed could triumph in the rocket-start rough house that characterises American sprinting. Straightaway our worst fears were realised. The gates opened and after two strides Dayjur was a length behind, with Willie Carson pumping desperately to gain a pitch.

Dayjur was drawn way out wide, 13 of 14. He was hard to see but he was moving through them. Yes, incredibly, as they ran through that scorching 21-second first quarter mile, it was Dayjur who worked his way up to settle on the hare-running leader Safely Kept.

But something had already gone wrong. So quick on first sight that the eye all but missed it. Horses and men were in the air. The massive Mr Nickerson had come down, the outsider Shaker Knit had fallen over him. Both were for the blood wagon. Jockey Chris Antley was for hospital with a collarbone fracture. But we only caught a glimpse. It was on the far side of the track, perhaps it had never happened. Concentrate on Dayjur.

We weren't to know that it was Dayjur who needed to do the concentrating. We were shouting now because Dayjur was alongside the big mare Safely Kept and had the legs of her. They were at the furlong pole. The sun was bright on Carson's flashing blue silks. Our camera went into close-up as he pulled his stick through into his right hand to give the little brown horse two back-handers for his final effort.

Carson got a response all right, the most brilliantly athletic response a thoroughbred has ever given. But, as we all know, it lost him the race. At 40 miles an hour Dayjur was capable of such a complete jump over a 20-foot shadow that he only lost half a length to the horse sprinting beside him. You could even say that he would have got back in front if he hadn't dropped at the larger bank of shadow just before the winning post.

Half an hour earlier or later the shadow wouldn't have been there. The day before we never even saw the sun. Willie Carson spoke for everyone as he shook his almost dirt-free head and said, "I just don't bloody believe it."

But on this day, once the script writer in the sky had dipped his nib in fantasy, nothing was impossible. Why, in the very next race Jose Santos came winging home on the hot favourite Meadow Star, just half an hour after he had been a bouncing jockey-ball when falling in the sprint. And then came Go For Wand.

The race went too perfectly to order. Bayakoa and Go For Wand head-to-head all the way. Into the straight and the whole stand is a cauldron of sound. Out on the track jockeys Pincay and Romero are whip-cracking dervishes with a hundred yards for the post. Then in one ghastly, cart-wheeling moment, Go For Wand was over and down.

Romero lay still, but the filly got up, and one look at the swinging right ankle told you the queen would become a carcass as soon as the vet could get the mercy-killing injection into her.

That's what happens at the racetrack. Somewhere, every week, almost every day. But this was centre stage, it was Breeders' Cup, it was Go For Wand. The place couldn't take it.

In her last moments the filly scrabbled, ankle swinging, across the course to the rails where the crowd was thickest, just 10 yards from our TV rostrum. A scarlet-coated, but cowboy-trained outrider galloped over, leapt from his pony to pull Go For Wand down like a steer out west. Women were screaming, granite-faced men were blubbing like children. For the Americans, it was all ruined, ruined utterly.

Yet for us it was not over and all the world knows why. Of course we had tremendous things at the close, Ibn Bey all but pulling off the Classic one race after In The Wings had sliced through his field in the Breeders' Cup Turf. But our day was saved by the oldest riding magician of all. As he and Royal Academy pulled up the commentator just gasped "Lester Piggott, who would believe it."

As the replay rolled on and on, you thought of all those other races down the years, the deadly stillness of the body as they run towards the turn, the inevitability of that finishing run, the last three machine gun cracks of the whip to print this richest and arguably greatest of all Piggott triumphs forever in the memory.

When he came across to do the TV interview they put the floodlights on him. His face had no need for illumination. After all the darkness, against all the odds, he was back. For us the day was back. Asked how at 54 he could still wave the wand, 12 days in from a five-year lay-off, he answered simply and with no need for false modesty.

"Ah no," he said, some Belmont mud still stuck in his teeth, "you never forget."

A greater comeback than Lazarus? Lester Piggott being interviewed at Belmont after his Breeders' Cup triumph on Royal Academy (Chris Smith)

3. Linked by One Obsession

Is obsession a dirty word? Sure, it invades the psyche,
it creates selfishness, narrowness and intolerance.
But it also gives a lift, a purpose, a vitality that
ordinary interests cannot match. Racing people are
obsessed all right.

Once caught, they work and live and die with it. It
gives a shape to their being, a method to their
madness, a drive to their dream, and all too often an
excuse for their failings.

One autumn afternoon in 1984, the signs of promise
were too obvious to miss.

A face in the frame
September 30th 1984

The nights are colder now. Racing thoughts turn to the jumping game, and the good news is that there's at least one new face in the family which might see something special before winter's out.

Early-season euphoria, perhaps, but important too. For these first two jumping months of the season have had to contend with more than the usual neglect in flat-racing's shadow. Champion jockey John Francome has farmed things almost to monopoly dimensions. He and trainer John Jenkins have had more than 30 winners, their nearest rivals hardly double figures. The rider plans to retire in June, so the thought at Fontwell on Wednesday was, "Could there be life after Francome?"

It's long been clear that, when he goes, the crinkly-haired record-breaker will leave a gap that no one generation of jockeys can fill. So it's to the younger men we look for fresh excitement, and at the grave risk of cashing in on coincidence I have to report that watching Richard Dunwoody at Fontwell was like seeing a champion in chrysalis.

Dunwoody is a 20-year-old with just one full amateur season behind him, riding experience with his ex-trainer father in Northern Ireland and flat-race polish from Newmarket. He's now a professional attached to Tim Forster's yard near Wantage. Off a horse, he still affects an unsophisticated modesty as if he were a junior member of the Young Farmers' Barn Dance Committee. Yet when he drove Sundiata home in the four-year-old hurdle on Wednesday, he not only landed a gamble for his connections, he looked the classiest thing on view.

All sports recognise the quality. It's when a player can conduct himself through the maelstrom of the game (or race, or match) as if moved by a superior intelligence. At a place like Fontwell, with a switchback figure-of-eight track which doubles as a jockey's nightmare and a spectator's

Overleaf: Lester Piggott's first win at Newmarket after his comeback (Chris Smith)

dream, you can see it very clearly. Even the first-rate journeymen jockeys on Wednesday often looked in a muddling, hustling hurry as they jostled around the ever-changing camber and turns. But Dunwoody, cool and forward-poised, blending beautifully with the movement of his horse, was different. He had class written all over him.

But even that is not the most important quality. The ability to win is. At the moment, Richard Dunwoody screams at you as the most stylish recruit since the teenage Andy Turnell some 20 years ago. But with that come disadvantages, not least the near impossibility of being as good as you look.

So while a battered old cynic like me watched with joy at the flair with which Richard picked his way round on Pompous Prince in the selling chase, I also noticed that for all the dark goggles, white mittens and thrusting flat-race finish, at the line he was still only second to City Marathon ridden by that tough if Sloane Ranger-sounding pilot, Penny Ffitch-Heyes.

More doubt still when Dunwoody's next ride, on the ironically named Famous Footsteps, looked equally stylish until they got to the open ditch. Famous Footsteps sidestepped on landing and Richard, perfect posture, black gloves for black colours and all, went humiliatingly out of the side door.

The rising star. Richard Dunwoody's potential shone out like a beacon in the autumn of 1984 (Chris Smith)

It's necessary to stress the chinks of fallibility, not to decry the man, but to emphasise how wide is the gap between whiz-kid and the champion. Ross Arnott, Peter Dever, Stan Moore and Jimmy Duggan will be making youthful headlines too, but none of them has quite the credentials of this young man, whose 26 amateur victories included an astonishing 800-1 four-timer at Hereford last April.

Some senior jockeys still assess him as "just a nice kid, who's coming on", but most will heed Tim Forster's carefully chosen words: "It's all very early yet, but if we go through the next couple of years, the sky could be the limit."

That's when you take a final memory from Fontwell: Sundiata is coming to the final flight carrying not just Dunwoody but the owner's (and your correspondent's) wages. The challenge has been timed perfectly, but the horse then ducks towards the crowd. He still wins. Not thanks to polish or style, but to something inside his rider that will not be denied.

Richard Dunwoody is now on the most ruthless treadmill in sport. He carries great gifts with him, but will be done no favours. How he and other young hopefuls manage should warm the winter through.

The record books already show that Richard has fulfilled that potential in spades. More than 500 winners, the Grand National with West Tip, the Gold Cup with Charter Party, the King George and other dazzling races with Desert Orchid.

Yet in some ways his achievements are a case of fulfilling what his family if not nature herself intended. Ron Thompson has had to chart a very different route. But who is to say that the obsession is any less pervading?

Where do racing trainers come from? Down the pit
January 27th 1985

When Ron Thompson came up from the pit to start a new life in the haulage business, he went to see his bank manager for a £500 loan. It didn't go well. "Without any assets, I can't help you, Mr Thompson," sniffed Old Stoneface. In exasperation, Ron put his great miner's hands on the table, and said: "But I have got these, and you have a vault full of stuff in there. Give me the loan, and you'll never regret it."

Ron got his money. With it he bought 10 lorry-loads of coal, sold the stuff in manageable small bags at a profit and, working all the hours God

gave to Cain, built up a big enough operation to be able, three years ago, to leave his son in charge. Now he's the unlikeliest thing in this Sunday's Britain, the miner who became a racehorse trainer.

Not a flashy "watch them from the Mercedes" trainer, mind. Thompson's unfinished breeze-block stables are still deep in mining country six miles from Doncaster at the back of Stainforth's aged Democratic Club, and next to a South Yorkshire "Steptoe" who lives in an old railway carriage and specialises in broken window-frames. The colliery is over there past the disused dog-track, and the nearest thing to a negotiated settlement is a pair of cows in the barn taken as part payment of one owner's training dues.

The world knows that up here the mining communities are struggling with the effects of 10 months on strike. But others also have their problems, and there have been plenty of worries in the northern part of the racing family. This month's Howard Wright survey in *Pacemaker* magazine showed

Up from under. Former miner Ron Thompson stands proud with his string in South Yorkshire (Chris Smith)

that during the 1984 flat-racing season, the north's 15 racecourses had over half their races and two-thirds their prize-money taken by horses trained south of Cambridge, and of the 80 top-rated two-year-olds last season, only one was based in the north.

There may be million-dollar yearlings at Newmarket and Lambourn, but up here the bloodstock bonanza is something you only read about in the newspapers.

The most expensive horse you'll meet at Haggswood Stables cost £5,000, and the stable star, a corkscrew-legged old gelding called Kindred, just £800. On Wednesday, the frost was on the ground, the flood still in the sand gallop, and as two of the seven-strong staff had just departed, your correspondent was press-ganged into riding out all morning. This surely was scraping the bottom of the racing barrel.

But you don't need to give lectures in barrel-scraping to a man who worked underground for eight years at Armthorpe (and once caused a three-day strike for refusing to obey a union walk-out). Nor are pontifications much use to a Doncaster lad whose handful of winners as a jockey came after he had started at age 13 with a local trainer, Eddie Magner, for the solid financial reason that the 7s 6d on offer was half-a-crown more than he got for delivering the groceries.

(Photo: Chris Smith)

"I have no inhaybations in having a go at the training game," says Ron, with one of those delightful malapropisms with which he sprinkles his Yorkshire chat. "The crucifix of the matter is to give value for money. I can do it for £70 a week (half the charge of a big Newmarket stable), because we have built the place ourselves. We work very hard, and I don't charge any extras. I have 23 boxes now, but I am sure I can fill 40 by the end of the season. Last year I had a lot of nom-de-plumes, but this time we have some nice two-year-olds."

And they have to bet. "I can't think of anyone, except perhaps the Queen, who doesn't need some wages out of this racing business," says Ron, adding with his spade-is-a-spade directness: "I don't like to bend the rules, but obviously when you're getting a horse fit for his first win, you're not telling everything to Joe Public. I aim to get 70 per cent of my 'touches' successful."

Sharing in all that on Wednesday was the head lad, Gordon Blackwell, miner's son Dean Lockwood and two slightly baffled girls from the Manpower Services Commission who, through some bureaucratic nonsense, are not allowed to start work until 8a.m., thereby missing a vital part of the stable day. That's not something you could ever throw at Ron's jockey daughter, Jayne, whose seven wins this season have included a brilliant defeat of Phil Tuck. A print of the photo-finish, inscribed by her victim, "Well done, Jayne, next time I will slip up your inner," hangs on the wall.

Jayne's special relationship (through five successes) has been with Kindred, who by this time was carrying me behind the stable's big two-year-old hope, Penrhyn Lad, as we hacked around the old quarry Ron uses as a warm-up track. Kindred started his career at Vincent O'Brien's equine Eton at Ballydoyle. It would be interesting to know what he makes of Thompson's slightly less manicured facilities. From the feel of him, as we later cantered endlessly round a ploughed field, and from the gleam in his coat, Kindred thought it was good to be alive.

If the old brute was ungrateful enough to suggest otherwise, he might ponder one final thought from South Yorkshire. Without men like Ron Thompson, there has, historically, been only one place for horses like Kindred and (once upon a time) for the people who work around him. Underground.

*In a few pages' (and 22 months') time I have to
relate how terrible a price Ron Thompson's family
had to pay for their racing involvement. But for many
of us there was an earlier bereavement. It hit deep.
It was the end of a friendship, the final passing of
youth.*

Mace the Ace
May 26th 1985

We used to call him "Mace the Ace", and no one deserved a dirty deal less. After a long and cruel illness Macer Gifford died on Thursday.

Anyone who has seen a sufferer from motor-neurone disease (the same affliction that killed David Niven in 1983) will appreciate that "blessed release" is no understatement. So the overwhelming sadness that still hit the former jockey's friends last week demands more than a passing explanation.

Of course, there was the first shock of how close death's spectre stalks. Gifford was just 40, and if that's going to be the time for cashing in chips, many of us are already overdue at the Pearly Gates and are certainly going to need "Mace" to put St Peter into a forgiving mood.

But that's only identifying a personal fear. This bereavement also spotlights a wider worry. It's a sense that everything has got too complicated, too money-conscious to be enjoyed. For the 15 years that he was around, to meet Macer Gifford was to know that life was for living.

He became a cracking good jockey. Never quite the standard of his brother Josh (champion four times between 1962 and 1968) but a man who didn't look out of place in the highest class and whose 230 winners (including the 1968 Whitbread Gold Cup on Larbawn) did not come by mistake. But his appeal to public and professionals alike was an innate warmth and friendliness that made him a cavalier in the truest sense.

He started as an amateur, and although he turned professional after topping the unpaid list in 1965, he never lost his initial boyish, tail-wagging enthusiasm for the game. Sceptics might point out that with 700 acres in Huntingdonshire which he used to farm with his Uncle George, Macer could afford to laugh at life. But those of us who rode with him through the sixties and seventies will remember something much stronger than that.

For several seasons Macer used to change next to Graham Thorner, never a man to have one worry when ten more might be available. "I remember one day very clearly," said Graham last week. "Everything had gone wrong, horses falling, trainers complaining, shoulders aching, and I said to him: "Look, Macer, you've got the farm and everything at home. Why the hell do you go on with this business?" He gave me a disbelieving look and said, 'But I love it all. The horses, the people, the gas, the life.' "

Macer's wonderful wife Sarah won't mind me saying that in earlier times Mr Gifford also had a healthy bachelor's appetite. My yellowing form book says that 20 years ago this week Macer and I were knocking around such Midland high spots as Uttoxeter and the now long-defunct Birmingham racecourse. It was only a winter or two later that we took two partners to some London ball. At about one in the morning Gifford put his ruddy farmer's face out into a white and freezing Park Lane, announced that

Sandown that afternoon was out of the question, and returned to the revels. He awoke just an hour before the first race to find the snow had melted, and only a very late cancellation saved some tricky explanations.

On evenings like this Macer tended to wear some velvet-collared jacket of his grandfather's and much of his style of life—hunting, coursing, carousing, working—had such a 19th- or even 18th-century yeoman's ring to it that you almost imagined him clattering up to the door like some long-coated, heavy-booted figure out of *Tom Jones*, rather than cruising up in the little Mercedes he got for winning on Larbawn.

Such harping back might just be melancholy if it was not for the other feeling that came through at Goodwood before Gifford's death was announced on Thursday. It was a beautiful day high on the Chichester Downs, and there was the usual huffing and puffing about Classic trials you get at this time of year. But something was missing.

It was as if, in their drive for results, the tiny band of professionals at the heart of the matter had lost their ability to transmit the enjoyment of what, for 99 per cent of those who follow it, is just a sport. Of course the sport is also a business but above all else it's a business to be enjoyed, and at a time when the public interest in racing, both in newspapers and on television, is being questioned as never before, some Gifford-style warmth and enthusiasm must come through.

For Macer Gifford left a message. It's not just performance that counts. It's people.

Macer was gone but Tim Forster survived. There was suddenly a need to touch base on where we began. There were good reasons for going.

Pessimism and perfection personified
January 1986

In the great panoply of racing pessimists there's no one to match Tim Forster. Before Ben Nevis's Grand National his last words to Charlie Fenwick were "keep remounting". Before Last Suspect this April, his only plans were to meet back at the weighing room "after we have caught him".

Once upon a long time ago, I was riding a horse for him at about 10-1 on in a two-runner race at Folkestone. That morning all he could say was "by a supreme piece of strategy, I have engineered a race that even a donkey couldn't lose, so try and avoid wrestling the wretched thing to the ground."

That has always been his style since he started his career as the oldest 24-year-old to ever saddle a winner. The statistics claim he wasn't 50 until last year but those of us who have known him a while don't believe that detail for a second. Tim Forster was born aged about 45, with a tweed cap on his head, a tall, cryptic, world-weary eye, and a cough on the end of his sleeve.

It was exactly 20 years ago this jumping season that I first left Wantage on the little road that winds through the Letcombes, and found myself so unaccountably and uncharacteristically early that I drove on up Sincom Hill towards Lambourn and took a beginner's step on that high downland terrain that was made to train jumping horses.

The anniversary trip this October reverted to a more typical schedule. A puncture on the M4 had me 40 minutes late and so the greeting when I finally bumped the old Land-Rover along the Ridgeway to catch Forster and his string at the misty top of Green Down, was not unanticipated . . . "I have always hated change," he called. "It would be terrible if you had been on time."

The surprise was not just the sense of *déjà vu*, but that the picture actually seemed, if anything, rather better than before. That's saying something because the place and the horses had always been a painter's dream, and because Forster, who had always been something of a physical wreck, was struck down last year by multiple sclerosis.

Yet in this early October light, the old downs looked even more ravishing and cared for than I remembered them all those mornings long ago. There was an elegant wood chip gallop beside the usual working ground up on Folly's Clump. The horses seemed dangerously close to the traditional pre-season boast "the best lot we've ever had". And Tim Forster looked within spitting image of being "in the pink".

It was as if the onset of his all-too-real affliction had given a new serenity. For years he has sat in his book-lined memento-laden bachelor den, picking at bars of chocolate, smoking like a chimney, and imagining himself to have every ailment in the book.

Now he has an actual problem and, admittedly with some reluctance, has forced himself to do something about it. Cigarettes have been eliminated and once a week he goes into a new low-pressure chamber at nearby Harlow, one of the latest devices to be used in the battle against multiple sclerosis.

"Of course it's really only cutting out the cigarettes," he says, prodding the walking stick into what must be one of the oldest and most cosseted turf gallops in the kingdom. "I have put on a bit of weight in the face and everyone keeps on coming up and saying how well I look. But the low-pressure chamber (it's like putting you 15 fathoms down in a diving bell) does give some relief, and the other people going through it are absolutely marvellous."

Complaints used to be an almost excessive part of the act—lack of prize-money, lack of suitable owners, of staff, of suitable races. If you had taken a pound for every time he had said, "That's it then, I will never train another winner," you would have crashed out in Krugerrands long ago. Nowadays the moans are more token than real. At times, Tim Forster even looks in severe danger of being a happy man.

Naturally, he would hate to admit it. We had plenty of stuff of how bad it was that his friends have so many children "that they can't afford the training fees", how impossible it was to buy a decent jumping sort, even of how quite unreasonable the good Lord was being with the excessively dry weather.

But see the horses file past the church and turn right for the climb up to the downs. Watch the string canter up to the skyline, a perfect evocation of Masefield's line "to keep the spirit free and the body lithe". Finally, look at the walls of triumphant photos including those three Grand Nationals and you know that Tim Forster has done that cleverest of tricks . . . by loving an institution he has actually become part of it.

To get the best out of jump racing you have got to like character and to take your time, both with the humans and with the horses. So it is that this man whose idea of a day out is to go fox-hunting on foot and to listen to the farmers jawing about crop rotations and calf subsidies, has always relished and even attracted the absurd tale, the eccentric spirit.

The Grand National stories are already well chronicled; Well To Do whose dam cost tuppence ha'penny and whose owner, the heavenly Heather Sumner, died tragically young of cancer leaving the horse to Forster; Ben Nevis, the pony-sized American timber horse who was supposed to detest the heavy going he faced at Aintree; Last Suspect, the talented old lag who had pulled himself up on his last run before Liverpool.

But there were many others. Old Baulking Green, jogging all day at the head of the string, the first, the 50th and the 100th of the 900-odd winners already logged. Mr Wonderful, the black bull of a horse whose speciality was to back towards you and deliver a right and left that would take a title in one. The Manse, an enormous thing so tall he must have been half giraffe, and so thin that we had to put on about six non-slip pads to prevent the saddle sliding over his tail.

Today's team, once again 50-strong despite all those claims of imminent disaster, has got its full share of odd-balls. There's Drumadowney, so crackers that he does both his work and his racing right out on his own. Western Sunset, the one-time brilliant novice who was cured of a dust allergy by the old countryman's wheeze of hanging a string of onions in his box. "Everyone laughed at first," says Forster with that wry look that signals amusement. "But now they keep ringing up asking what sort of onions they should use." There is Royal To Do, the last of Well To Do's half-brothers who was so athletic when schooling last year that he somehow managed to get his front leg through the neckstrap on his martingale.

But, while the individual stories may differ, the type of horse is just the same as ever. Big strapping yeomen who come marching out with solid tread, massive great shoulders and strong masculine necks. After a summer of watching flat racing, this lot seem like a team of beefy rugby players and make their million-dollar counterparts in the other game seem like little flash-suited soccer men.

Some of them will be too slow to score many points and it's ironic that quite a few of the best winners, Loup Cervier, Royal Marshall, New Boy and Salvador, have come from a smaller mould. But Forster will go on getting the big fine horses because "the exceptions don't disprove the rule. You need a man's horse to go chasing."

The type may remain. So too do many of the people. Head Lad John Humphrys has been there from the very beginning. Humphrys remains a workaholic although he has allowed a rare glimpse of sunlight into life by no longer adding the grind of daily riding out to his many other duties. It would be too much to ask Travelling Head Lad Peter Feltham to carry anything lighter than a furrowed brow in public but privately he now sees the absurd side too and there is still no better indication of a winning chance than when the Feltham tenner is on.

On the female side, Gill Kermac now does a noble Girl Friday stint and Marigold Coke has been managing the office with quiet efficiency for years. It's five years since Hwyel Davies was signed up for as only the fourth jockey since Forster started and there are those who can't remember a couple of slap-happy years when B Scott rode in support of the indomitable G Thorner. Who would dare to suggest that, with Richard Dunwoody as a back-up to Davies. Tim Forster now has unquestionably one of the most talented and powerful saddle teams of jump racing.

Yet, while it's all very well to develop this ultimate of jumping ships with which to sail the steeplechasing ocean, the trouble is that this autumn, as so often, the hard ground has stopped it putting to sea. By the end of November Forster had run only eight of his 50 horses and with masochistic gloom was saying, "It's quite ridiculous. We are almost half-way through the season. We'll probably be roughing horses off after Christmas and we've still hardly run a thing."

The frustrations are very real and are central to the jump trainer's life. Owners, lads, jockeys find the waiting hard to bear but with as established a team as Forster's the lessons have been painfully spelt out before. "I remember we ran a couple of really nice horses. Care and The Very Light, at Wincanton on Boxing Day. But the ground was firm and when they got home they both had a bit of a leg, had to be fired, missed a whole season. If you have big, fine horses like we have you have just got to wait until the ground comes for them."

When the late Peter Hastings heard that the young Forster was going to train he told Tim's mother, "Just make sure he doesn't end up with the jumpers. All those breakdowns will break his heart." Twenty-five years on the advice has been ignored but at times the prophecy has come all too near to reality.

"It might sound absurd," says Forster with a very genuine groan. "But from now until the summer I live with an obsession about horses' legs. Coming back from the races after we have worked horses in the morning I drive slower and slower as we get near Letcombe, just dreading what John's face will be like. I can tell within half a second if something is wrong. He says, 'I think you should come and see so and so's leg . . . I don't like the look of it,' and you know there is trouble."

"What's almost worse," adds the trainer, "is then having to go back and ring the owner. One is very lucky to have friends who are understanding when you have to tell them to abandon so much that they, and I, were looking forward to . . . a day out to Ludlow to see their horse run . . . a stop for a cup of tea on the way home."

Although he has won most of the big jumping prizes, it's noticeable that it's the smaller country tracks, the Wincantons, Tauntons, Ludlows, that slip easiest from the tongue. Horses were always far more likely to be despatched for some modest target at Hereford than to pitch in against heavyweights at Newbury. That's unlikely to change and neither is Forster's wish to fly the traditional jumping flag.

"I think it's very important to offer it as an alternative to the flat-racing business. After all, what we're suggesting is that going on a winter day out to Wincanton can be rather more fun than agonising whether your horse has had £25,000 knocked off its value by getting beaten, or agonising whether or not you can win some wretched little Group Race."

"The other great thing about jumping," he goes on, warming to his theme, "is that an owner can get much more involved with his horse. Professor Plum won his 18th race the other day. His owners have had him for 10 years, had him home each summer. Flat racing just cannot give you anything like that. My aim is to have horses and owners that last."

The illness might seem to put all that under threat but it has also given renewed incentive. "I am very lucky to live in a village," he says. "Everybody has been very kind and it is very rewarding to see how people in the village consider that our horses are their horses. And the other thing is that when you are feeling a bit moderate of a morning, the thought of 20 horses walking around beneath the window is a wonderful spur. I may not have been very good tempered sometimes. But I haven't missed a morning yet."

Tim Forster wouldn't like you to think it but they sounded a little close to the words of an optimist.

*Forster's team was cruelly hit when a heart-attack
killed John Humphrys in 1989. Yet Tim himself
continues on, wrapped in tradition like a blanket
against time. It's a garment that can last many a
winter. Just about the oldest user was still enjoying it
in his nineties.*

Vintage delights of being Jim Joel
February 16th 1986

When you can remember Buffalo Bill visiting your parents' country home
and Caruso singing at their house in Grosvenor Square; when your first
Derby memory is of Edward VII leading in Minoru; when you have survived
the Flanders mud and the Kimberley diamond fields to grace the smartest
end of the racing scene; when you are 91, as Jim Joel is now, you are
entitled to give the game a beady eye.

Understandably it's a rheumy old eye nowadays. But it's not a dull, nor
an unaffectionate one. Perhaps keener on the past than the present but still
strictly of today because at this moment he is one of the leading owners of
this jumping season and remains the only Englishman since the war (39–
45 this time!) to have topped the list in both the flat and National Hunt
codes.

Mr Joel's Door Latch is set to carry the famous black colours and scarlet
cap with a major chance in this year's Grand National and his unbeaten
Midnight Count is most people's idea of the nicest young horse they have
seen in ages. They are just two of the two dozen Joel keeps in training
but they are discussed with the opinionated enthusiasm of the one-horse
beginner.

So is much else, as he sips that wonderful first glass of champagne with
the snow blazing white outside the sitting room window. After all, Mr Joel
and his 20-mare Childwick Bury Stud just north of St Albans are living
history. It was founded by the Tottenham Court Road furniture king, Sir
Blundell Maple, was bought by Jim's father, Jack, who went out from the
East End of London to make a fortune in the South African diamond fields.
And while Jim now lives in what must be the best converted "semi" in
Britain (half a stud groom's cottage), the enormous original mansion
now houses the fevered imagination of the film director, Stanley "2001"
Kubrick.

Mr Joel is a small, reticent, slightly shrunken figure. His talk retains
the "old-boy" argot of an Edwardian childhood, just as the room has the
traditional sepia-photo clutter of shooting parties and Derby winners (Jack
had two, Sunstar in 1911 and Humorist in 1921; Jim as yet just one, Royal
Palace in 1967). But while age may wither it doesn't necessarily take away

The roll of the years. In his nineties, Jim Joel has plenty of racing honours to look back on (Chris Smith)

from wisdom, and the lesson this most experienced of all racing observers is keen to leave at the end of his innings is that if anyone is going into the expensive hassle of racehorse owning, it might as well be fun.

"Of course there's some good trainers around nowadays," he says, himself topping up the glasses while Alec the butler prepares lunch in the next room. "No man can train 200 horses, and I don't want to be just a number on a list of owners. I don't see why the Arabs don't get a private trainer like we did and Sangster is doing now with Michael Dickinson. You are just so much more involved, even more so when you have bred them yourself. Why, if we had runners-up at Liverpool, we would have dinner with Charlie Morton at the Adelphi at about seven and then go out in dinner-jackets to watch him feed the runners himself. Charlie used to feed all his horses, but then he never had more than 30 to worry about."

Whether today's high-tech, 100-horsepower trainers would appreciate Charlie's idea of an annual holiday—renting a house at Brighton for

Goodwood and the Sussex fortnight—any more than they would relish his "gobble-up" mealtimes, remains to be seen. But the Joel memories are now in full flood. The horror of the collapsed cab horses on the London hills. How he dodged cricket at Malvern: "We had some good animals racing and I told them I had to study The Form." How, despite that, his headmaster would not allow him to attend Sunstar's Derby. How they thought the ill-fated Humorist was ungenuine until his early death revealed tuberculosis. How his father rode round the stud on a white Egyptian donkey. How serious culling was needed to get the quality back after Jack Joel's death in 1940.

The driving energy and supposed meanness of the old man inhabits much of the conversation. "He would never give me anything, of course," says Joel minor, with his watery, lopsided, smile. "But I did get him to send me a decent horse to ride as a charger in 1916—Sirian, he had been second in the Middle Park Plate. Came up with the remounts from Rouen, went right through the war without turning a hair. We had a plan afterwards to train him for a race in Cologne, but the old man insisted that he come back to England and Charlie Morton won something with him at Nottingham."

Although Jim Joel has kept a much lower profile than his swashbuckling father, he has kept involved enough with the family fortunes still to go to his London office three times a week, and in the racing world he has left a deep impression. Not in administration but in his belief in caring for those around him. Much has been made of his quiet but considerable charity. "Just trying to do a good turn," he says, but it comes through strongest when he takes a walking-stick stroll among his staff. "I think if you're going to be in this racing game you've got to get all the chaps involved. Then the horses belong to everyone."

Josh Gifford trains Door Latch and Midnight Count who, along with the Henry Cecil-trained Two Thousand Guineas candidate, Brave Owen, could make it a memorable 92nd spring for Jim Joel. With magnificent directness and splendid disregard for English grammar, Josh pays all our tributes. "He's seen it all. He listens to it all. He lets you make up your own mind. I tell you something, he's learned me a lot."

A year after that article appeared Jim Joel added another entry to his story. Maori Venture won the Grand National in the famous black and scarlet colours, but before that not all changes were for the better.

It was a brilliant August morning when the news of Ryan Price's death came through on the radio. It had been expected but was now official. Written words are muted trumpets but sometimes you still want to blow farewell.

The lion's roar is stilled
August 17th 1986

The old lion will roar no more. Ryan Price died yesterday morning and for many of us racing will never be the same again.

It was his 74th birthday and although he had been desperately ill for some months the news still comes as a jolt.

For Ryan, the most colourful, outrageous, most brilliantly versatile trainer of his era, was above all else a life force that never wavered. He is gone. The wind blows cold from the north.

But let's remember the times when it gusted gloriously up from the south, later from Findon, but first from a tiny yard in Lavant, West Sussex, after Ryan had returned from France with a commando's MC, a captain's rank and tales of derring-do which must have made Hitler wish he had quit in the Sudetenland.

Jump racing was Price's original territory and for 25 years his horses tilted at the major prizes, winning the Grand National, the Cheltenham Gold Cup, the Champion Hurdle three times, and the Schweppes Hurdle on four controversial occasions. In the 1970s he had switched almost totally to the flat and took the Oaks (Ginevra), the St Leger (Bruni) and the Champion Stakes (Giacometti).

Yet, as with his jumping successes, it was the style rather than the mere statistics that made Ryan unforgettable. With his chiselled features set in arrogant concentration, his trilby at a rakish angle, he himself used to lead his horses, battle-primed out on to the track.

That fierce competitiveness and fearless confidence ("Of course he will bloody well win, this horse is a champion"), allied to his knack of winning when the money was down, led to inevitable clashes with the authorities.

He was banned for a year after Rosyth's second Schweppes victory and had to endure lengthy but finally unproven drug investigations after Hill House's Schweppes three years later.

Yet the bark was always far worse than the bite, and it was Ryan at home with his devoted wife Dorothy, and high on those Sussex Downs with his beloved horses that gave you the key to his genius.

When he retired in 1982 his health failed quickly and when I talked to him last month he was clearly dying. For a while there was only sadness, like some cold, burnt-out grate. Then another trainer's exploits were mentioned and I suggested that someone from Findon had been there before.

At last an ember glowed, a whisper grew almost to a chuckle and the captain said: "Ah, yes, old boy, and had a lot of fun doing it. A lot of fun." There should be quite a party at the Pearly Gates.

Father Time seemed to stalk too close in 1985.

At the end of the year he was knocking on the door
again. Would that he stuck to his schedule.

In anger and in grief, farewell to friends
November 16th 1986

Two deaths in the family this week, one sad, the other tragic. At 82, Gordon Richards had lived a fine span and a full one. Jayne Thompson was 60 years younger. When her life support machine was switched off on Friday our reaction wasn't just despair but anger.

For how good a game is this when it kills a delightful young woman and shatters her family? How splendid are we to praise the fun of places like Catterick when they turn into burial grounds? That is the rage of bereavement. The truth is that Jayne and most of the rest of us wouldn't share it for long.

For doubt not that Jayne died as she would have lived at the gallop and fulfilling her father's dream. Ron Thompson did shifts as a jump jockey before going down the mine for 10 years. When he had worked his way out and set his son up in the haulage business he returned to racing, and a visit to the training yard he has built in the shadow of Stainforth colliery near Doncaster was to see very much a family affair.

"She's just a natural," Ron would say with unconcealed pride. "Once she got her pony, this was what she wanted to do. We suggested other things but this was what she was good at, what she loved." Two years ago Jayne's nine winners made her the leading woman professional. Now she is another statistic, the first girl to be killed on a British racetrack. Her father's mare, Hot Betty, crashed at the first flight of Catterick's Skellfield Selling Hurdle last Saturday and fired Jayne's head so hard into the ground that even a fully fitted crash helmet couldn't prevent brain damage of terrible and fatal proportions.

On the face of it, the Thompsons, Catterick, and the Skellfield Selling Hurdle are as far as you can get from the record-breaking glories so well celebrated in Gordon Richards' obituaries last week. But, quite apart from the twist that his death on Monday was actually Jayne's 22nd birthday, let's remember that Gordon's father was a miner, and one of the mainsprings to that unique determination was that he too had a love, a hunger for the game.

Sir Gordon Richards may have walked with (and ridden for) kings and queens, but he didn't collect his 26 championships and 4,870 winners without being fully committed to Catterick and all other points of the racing compass. Indeed, it was this relentless season-long voyage around the country which was part of the charm which put him beyond the range of ordinary sporting heroes and into the galaxy of national institutions.

All through the recession-hit 1930s and war-torn 1940s the excellence of

"Gordon" (only the Christian name needed) was one of the few topics on which all walks of society could agree. For prince and pauper alike could recognise that here was someone not only special at his job (the newsreel clips this week have reminded us of that upright, loose-reined, whip-swinging style) but who was as genuine as the oak in Nelson's *Victory*.

For how many sportsmen say things like "a public position gives you public responsibilities" and actually act accordingly? How many swim through the swirling pools of pressure and high-profile exposure without a whiff of scandal? How many get out the other side with their money, modesty, and sense of humour intact? The great trainer, Noel Murless, now old and frail himself, got it right this week when he said gently: "Let's not talk of the jockey, let's talk of the man."

People forget that Gordon Richards was a self-generated phenomenon. With no racing background it took him six seasons to become a household name. For Lester Piggott, bred and raised to be champion jockey, it took just one schoolboy ride. People may not have stressed how this super-fit little dynamo suffered comparatively delicate health. Richards missed a season with TB in his early twenties and his autobiography records how his nerves several times worried him almost to collapse.

And no one could over-emphasise his old-fashioned devotion to his wife Marjorie. Her death from cancer three years ago broke him in two.

But that is what he was. Let's go back to what he did. A long time ago (probably August '52) Dad and I got on the train for Brighton races. In the carriage my father talked excitedly of some horse (exhumed form books suggest a Murless runner called Monarch More) who had disappointed last time out but whom Richards might regalvanise that day. We were going to watch "Gordon" ride.

Ten-year-old schoolboys don't always retain very much, but I can still see the tiny, square, rolling-gaited figure, small enough to be a tumbling circus clown if it hadn't been such solemn stuff as the great snorting horse was led up and the trainer finished his messages. Then suddenly the little man was in the saddle with four long legs beneath him and for the first time I saw the magic of a half-ton thoroughbred played by touch.

Some years on I had an infinitely less successful but marvellously exciting stab at the jockey's life. Nothing has ever replaced the thrill of the horse power underneath and the winning post ahead. I know why Jayne died. But it doesn't hurt any less.

Steve Cauthen has also been near the line. He too
knows the split second before oblivion. He has made an
incredibly lucrative deal with fame, but doubt not that
he has to pay for it.

The kid has it all—except happiness
April 2nd 1989

At first glance, Steve Cauthen's opening days back in the racing saddle have gone splendidly well. Seven and a half months after he broke his neck in a horrific fall at Goodwood, the 28-year-old American returned to business at Kempton and duly punched home a handsome colt called Ceciliano for the most popular winner of the week.

As he was led in, the smile was radiant with pride and relief. The brilliant career which has taken him from coast-to-coast teenage sensation in America to the very top of the European Classic tree, could gallop on to further glory.

This jockey's lot should be a happy one. In many ways Steve Cauthen has better prospects than any other sportsman in the land. Ten years and more than 1,000 winners on from his arrival at our shores, he has become accepted, stylish and greatly loved. His association with the Henry Cecil stable means he is supplied with some of the finest thoroughbreds ever foaled. His ability in the saddle, and his attractive personality out of it, have made him a much-needed ambassador for the racing game.

The strain of narrow vision. Only through self-denial can Steve Cauthen chase the glittering prizes (Chris Smith)

Yet it is odd to relate that the strongest impression after a few days tracking Kentucky's favourite son is of feeling slightly sorry for him. He doesn't ask for sympathy, and still has opportunities for sport and social pleasures. But his private persona tends to be a lot more withdrawn than the self-confident young master who walks towards the TV cameras. His is a life where the pressures give a very much darker side to the moon than the golden sunlight of Derby-Day success.

It's not just the physical danger and the dreariness of a sparrow's diet. After all, the wondrously buoyant Peter Scudamore has gone through his record-breaking jumping season on equally thin rations, and his 540 rides have included at least 20 full-pelt collisions with mother earth. For Cauthen on the flat, the crashes can be serious—there was a nasty moment when a leather broke on Thursday—but they are mercifully few and far between.

"I don't worry about the Goodwood fall," he said last week, "because I don't remember anything about it. But I have fallen before. I know what it's like hitting the dirt. I know what it's like to be trampled on. All you can do is stay alert and keep yourself in the best possible shape."

Despite his claim that he is still short of 100 per cent fitness, there's no doubt that Steve buckled down to his physical regime once he was finally cleared by the doctors in the early part of the year. After four unsuccessful rides on Thursday, his steady breathing was a tribute to the long course of exercise in the gym, on the road and at the training ground, that he has put himself through.

There's also no doubt that Cauthen in the saddle adds a dimension to the English scene. He bends his willowy 5ft 6in frame round a racehorse in a unique blending of local and American styles. His toes are hooked into the stirrup irons, the left leg deeper down the horse than the right; "acey deucey" they call it across the Atlantic. His body perches high and strong to balance his equine partners over the undulations which are a daily part of the British tracks.

Standing hard against the rails to watch him at Doncaster on Thursday was to relish the summer ahead, just as cricket fans must have done at the week's pictures of a new, skinny Ian Botham warming up in Singapore. Cauthen's elbows slowly pumping up to a winning-post crescendo are as good a thought as the thumping whack of that mighty Worcestershire bat.

Yet you can still get nearly two of Steve into Ian's new slimline frame, and when you realise that Thursday's Cauthen still has four pounds to pare off a fairly hungry body, you know why this jockey's life has no beer and few skittles.

Time was when Steve got by on the more traditional "dine now, waste later" method adopted by riders down the centuries, but this and the odd glass of champagne began to ruin his metabolism. He ended 1985 in a clinic, and today his focus on the positive still carries clear elements of the one-day-at-a-time war he has had to declare on normal appetites.

"The dieting is simple," he said rather mournfully, "but it's never easy. A jockey just has to accept it as part of his life." He was talking on the car phone while the big Jaguar thundered towards Newmarket in the hands of John Barnes, his dignified ex-policeman chauffeur, whose earlier honours once included guard duty outside No. 10.

The present Cauthen abode, a tiny lodge-gate cottage on the Stetchworth Park Stud, is a far cry from Downing Street, and while it is obviously an escape from the back-slapping bonhomie of racecourse life, some nights it must seem like a prison cell in the empty hours after Barnes has left to join his wife and children.

Scudamore may have to take far greater risks for only a fraction of the money, but the thought of him reading stories to his two sons back in the Cotswolds leads to the conclusion that he has the better deal at present.

Maybe a degree of imprisonment is necessary. Sophistication can be an enemy to the tunnel vision a sportsman needs. Cauthen has tasted and enjoyed the bright lights, and his reaction to the pressures they brought has been to remain very close to his parents across the water. A day never goes by without a call coming in from Tex or Myra, his greatest supporters.

Some of Steve's friends say all he needs is a nice girl and a game of golf, but if you are young and glamorous and yet value your privacy, the answer is not always that easy.

Cauthen himself reverts to some old Kentucky wisdom as he faces the season ahead.

"The grass is always greener on the other side," he said a shade wistfully, his long, birdlike nose puckering back in concentration. "Sometimes you fly to Rome on a Sunday and look at other people and think that their life is much more carefree. But the guy who runs the corner store has his problems. I work with a team to get the horses ready. My part I can only do by myself, and I have to motivate myself."

Then, with a firmness that should worry rivals and delight fans, he added: "I guess I must have succeeded or I wouldn't be back to start all this again."

Don't let's worry overmuch for Cauthen. He may have to exist on starvation rations through the season, but life can't be all bad when you have got contracts with Sheikh Mohammed for business and with Amy Rothfuss for intended matrimony. He has won most of the battles. He has set the example for younger jockeys to follow. Step forward the next generation.

The boy wonder with the right breeding
July 2nd 1989

He crouches low, he is going fast, but history shows that Frankie Dettori's game could also be snakes and ladders.

The winners are coming on the flood—30 already this term, a dozen in the last fortnight. The phone is ringing, the praise is lavish, the smile is easy. At 18, Frankie is the season's teenage shooting star. But can he, against the trend, continue the climb to the very top of the board?

The facts are not encouraging. Since a youthful Pat Eddery led the table in 1971, no other champion apprentice has made it to the highest class. Philip Robinson ('79, '80) won a title this year, but that was in Hong Kong. Over here, Kevin Darley ('78), Richard Quinn ('84) and Michael Hills ('83) are having good seasons just outside the top 10 (and behind Dettori), but

Streamlined to the top. Frankie Dettori aiming for the highest targets in 1989 (Chris Smith)

some of the others have found the going much tougher.

Robert Edmondson ('72) and David Dineley ('76) both got beaten by the weight, and have stopped completely, while yesterday morning's chart showed that Alan Bond ('75, '76) had scored just once this term, Jimmy Bleasdale ('77) twice and poor Gary Bardwell only three times, already far removed from the patronage which made him champion apprentice in both the last two seasons.

In a very real sense, these lads have been victims of their own success. It is too easy to be hailed as racing's boy wonder. Obviously they all ride well and bubble with confidence, but the main reason they boot home winners is that they are "flavour of the month", and are given good horses to steer.

The precocious soccer star or cricketer gets nothing like it. Just because Dettori has caught fire, everybody wants to load him up on "buzzers", many of which would collect whoever was on board. They are racing's equivalent of the long hop offered to batsmen and, since apprentices get a weight allowance until they have ridden 75 winners, the young riders are playing with a bigger bat.

As this process goes on, we bow-legged hacks usually start to describe the new prodigy as the greatest talent in decades. That is fun while it lasts, but it builds up unreasonable expectations in the profession and often in the youth himself. A year on from the apprentice title, he has to be properly measured against his seniors, and if a couple of results go against him the "boy trying to do a man's job" whisper goes round, and on to the snake he goes just as the next over-hyped wunderkind starts scampering up another ladder.

The truth is that experience is so vital a part of a flat-race jockey's craft that he does not mature until his late twenties, is in full bloom in his thirties and can continue in splendour almost to the half-century. So what chance has young Frankie of avoiding a ride down the reptile's back?

The odds may be against him, but at this stage there are some hard reasons for suggesting that Dettori could be the exception. He is the right size—5ft 4in and lean and lithe at 7st 12lb. He has the right attitude and talent, and his connections and breeding are for the Classic game.

Since the Second World War, no young star has had a stable behind him of the size and power of Luca Cumani's 150-horse Derby-winning yard in which Dettori works at Newmarket. And, even more significantly, not since Pat Eddery has the year's top apprentice been the son of a champion. Frankie Dettori is heir to a legend.

Not in England of course, although Dettori senior made his Classic mark here with back-to-back Two Thousand Guineas wins on Bolkonski and Wollow for Henry Cecil in 1975 and 1976. But in his native Italy, Gianfranco Dettori has ruled the roost for years and years, and he won their Two

Thousand Guineas this spring at the age of 49. Talks with Dettori minor never go very far before "my father" enters the conversation.

The importance of this is hard to exaggerate. For most boys the fact of riding just one winner is enough to swell the chest and dazzle the parents. For Dettori it is the family profession, and it shows. "When I was 14," he explained at Kempton on Wednesday, "my father said, 'You have got the talent, and I can give you the chance to go and ride in England and in France to see how you like it.' I came here and I liked it."

While Frankie has inherited the warm and rubbery smile which is his father's sole means of communication with the British media, he has also developed a multi-layered Anglo-Italian accent which must be the linguistic version of the Neapolitan ice cream. But beneath the charm there is already an astute professionalism that could serve him well.

"Last year I was too weak," he said bluntly. "After spending four months during the winter riding for Richard Cross, I started this season feeling much stronger, but in a way I was trying too hard. I remember being second in one race at Thirsk in April, and I felt, and looked, as if I was going faster than the horse. That weekend I had a long think, and have tried to get more rhythm now."

It is certainly coming. The 30th winner was on a blinkered old thinker called Say You Will at Lingfield on Friday. There was a lot to like in the Cauthen-modelled low-backed poise which brought the horse through, and in the inspiration that enabled them to hang on in a photo-finish.

But there were rough edges, too, moments of indecision as to whether to hit or push as the opponent closed and his own horse weakened. The real excitement of watching Frankie Dettori is not what he can do today, but what he might do in the years ahead. If the snakes don't bite.

Dettori has hardly taken a backward step since those words were written. With more than 100 winners in 1990, his first big-time season, he is already part of the furniture. It won't be long before he is up the stairs.

His has so far been a gilded route to success but be sure that the snakes still slither offering temptation, deviation or just simple, malicious, tongue-flickering gossip.

That last is the most intrusive reptile of all. Ask Martin Pipe. Two hundred and fifty winners in the 1989–90 season was a bit like a first division team finishing 30 points clear in the football league. Yet all the while his rivals were keener to carp than to copy. A journey to Somerset might have shown them what they were missing.

The winning wonders of Martin Pipe
January 7th 1990

When will the losers learn? Despite the daily evidence, there are still some people afraid of the most revolutionary truth to come out of racing for many a decade: that in training terms Martin Pipe has all but re-invented the wheel.

"It suits us fine," Pipe's stable jockey, Peter Scudamore, said of the disbelief and even resentment of Pipe's success felt by jealous outsiders.

For whatever others may think, the winners continue to roll for Pipe, the Taunton bookie's son, with Chester Barnes, the former table tennis star, as wise-cracking aide-de-camp and driver of Pipe's blue Rolls (the one with the personalised registration number MCP1).

"Every day that people fail to recognise what he is doing," Scudamore

(Photo: Chris Smith)

said, "he goes further ahead, and they have more ground to catch up."

These are strong words for the wise and sober Scudamore and there were more to come. "So many people are governed by the old values," he said of reaction to the usual Pipe pace-setting tactics, "that they are not prepared to admit to change. They have a very old-fashioned, very British approach."

Scudamore's own conversion came some five years ago when he was told by Pipe that he was riding "the biggest certainty of the day" and he should make all the running. "You must be joking," Scudamore said, having known the animal at its previous stable. "He wouldn't get the trip in a bus." Pipe insisted, the partnership clicked, and the rest has become racing history.

That sort of tale embodies the central strength of the Pipe system—aggressive tactics, fitter horses, and hittable targets. "Very early on," he said in his clipped but unbombastic West Country voice, "I realised there were only two reasons why horses didn't win. They were either in the wrong race or they were not fit enough. It's taken a long time, but we have now got a very good team."

At 44, he is still a fox: quick, inquisitive and uncatchable despite a limp which ended a short and singularly unsuccessful riding career in 1973. It has turned into legend how he gradually changed a run-down old farm near Wellington into a 100-horse factory of winners, with the most efficient facilities in the country. But it is essential to know where and for how long he has been building.

"Look," he says, "I'd never got on to a horse until I was 18 and then I promptly fell off the other side. When we started with point-to-pointers I didn't know anything except for bookmaking. I'd never even worked in another yard. So I just read books, tried to analyse and carried on from there. We are only just beginning. There are so many things we don't know about the workings of a horse."

It has taken time to evolve today's record-breaking system from the cheap little selling hurdlers of the early years. Pipe started in 1974. It took him until 1979 to get into double figures for a season, and until 1983 to get out of the twenties.

But a visit to the functional breeze-block yard at the foot of the Blackdown Hills shows how the old betting-shop pragmatism has gone to work.

In particular those original reasons for not winning have been addressed. Finding the right race was never going to be that difficult with his bookmaking background and with the form expert Roy Hawkins as a full-time guide, but it is when you study how Pipe tries to get horses fitter that the equation suddenly adds up.

All his much-vaunted additions, such as the laboratory, the weighbridge, the gait-measurer, the swimming pool, the horse-walker and the newly built covered ride, only serve as marvellously well-organised checks and balances

to the one facility that practically every other trainer has more of: the gallops.

Pipe's gallops consist of one six-furlong wood-based strip up the side of a bank. It's up this that the horses breeze, hack back and repeat. In essence, Pipe has cracked interval training.

Not that he will make any such grandiose claims. He talks merely of giving horses "short, sharp bursts to keep their enthusiasm without strain". He speaks of different sorts of exercise to keep them active in body and fresh in mind, above all he talks of the need to have weekly, sometimes even daily, logging of blood and weight patterns to analyse their well-being.

It is this last which has led to scurrilous rumours of everything from frequent collapse to "blood doping", but the distinguished vet Bill Walter has known the yard from the inside since the point-to-pointing days. "Such talk is either ignorant or jealous or often both," he said. "These horses are very well looked after.

"For a start this isn't any old all-weather gallop. They put down three and a half thousand tons of stone before the special woodchip topping, which means the surface is always the same. Martin has built a programme in his mind for getting his horses fit. He works his horses hard but with his genius for organisation he uses his staff and his blood tests as his safety valve and they get fewer problems than many other teams.''

Seeing is believing and watching the Pipe horses thundering three-abreast up and down that bank last week made the logic of his attack devastatingly simple. If you could get horses to accept more intensive training without banging up their legs or blowing out their minds you would have a harder, fitter instrument than the racehorse prepared on methods which have changed little in 50 years.

If you have that fitter horse, what's the point of risking defeat for lack of pace in a race? "People say if you make the running you will 'blow up','' Pipe said. "What's 'blow up' mean other than that a horse is unfit? We only take them to the racecourse if they are ready to gallop all the way.''

So we have reached the present phenomenon. Practically every day of the jumping season you will see the blue and red MCP rug stripped off and there will be the latest Pipe runner. Whatever the race it will probably be favourite. It will be hard, lean and ready.

"They actually look different,'' Scudamore said. "The one time I remember seeing something similar was when I went to Sandown last flat season and saw one of Henry Cecil's. It was Indian Skimmer before the Eclipse.''

Which begs a final question. Now that Pipe's system has taken him to the very top of the jumping tree, will not the greater competition but infinitely richer rewards of flat racing beckon?

"We don't have the sheikhs or any of the big owners down here,'' Pipe said swiftly. "You can't plan these things, but if something turned up I would accept the challenge.''

Who knows where the revolution may have spread by the end of the century?

Martin Pipe is an astounding but self-made
phenomenon. Lester Piggott is a natural, a genius,
a freak. He has always drawn the drama towards him
yet by the autumn of 1990 most of us had accepted that
the only big story left to write about him was his
obituary. He was approaching his 54th birthday, he was
five years out of the saddle and two out of jail.
Then he stunned us all. He was coming back.

Rider in restless pursuit
October 14th 1990

It was all that we hoped for and all that we feared: a picture, last December from Lima, Peru. It showed Lester Piggott, in full jockey kit, alongside the local "Numero Uno". There was a smile on that lined old face we hadn't

The lines of Lester. Mr Piggott awaiting the call (Chris Smith)

seen since his official retirement in 1985. Only on horseback could he seek a happy ending.

After that sudden, South American appearance and the nationwide acclaim of two celebrity races in Ireland this summer, perhaps we should not have been surprised at Thursday's news that Lester was to ride again. And those of us who say, "He must be crackers," forget that his principal motivation is to avoid going mad with boredom.

On Friday he was not bored. He was bronzed and fit and ready for action. His ranch-style house and stables at the southern end of New-market have seen many a press stake-out these last five years, but all of them for non-racing reasons as a golden career ended in tragedy and disgrace. Suddenly the cameras and notebooks were back at the gate, the phone was under siege; and this time they were back for the longest-running refrain in sport: "What will Lester ride?"

He was in his swimming-trunks beside the pool, even at 54 his lean, tightly muscled torso a rebuke to the passing years. He has had a longstanding love–hate relationship with the media ever since he first made the head-lines 40 years ago: proud of his achievements, but resentful of the publicity given to his more turbulent side. Now there was no doubting the old gun-slinger's satisfaction that he was back into the game where he calls the shots. "I feel fit," he said dismissively. "Why not give it a go?"

Piggott back, history renewed. It is an intoxicating thought, yet he joins a long list of stars who could not find any substitute for the dazzling, sweat-stinging, fulfilment of their particular sporting stage. At first the *aficionados* love it, an unexpected sighting of the waxwork made life. But then dis-appointment sets in as they see the magic is no longer there, the mind making appointments the body cannot meet. Nobody believes that this will happen to Lester. Or rather, they do not want to.

For no one can exaggerate the length and the power of the Piggott legend in the racing game. This is no ordinary champion: this is the most brilliant, difficult, abiding genius that any century will ever see. He rode his first winner as a pudgy-faced 12-year-old in August 1948. Four days earlier, Don Bradman had been out for a duck at the Oval and, just a month before that, the Health Service had been invented. Someone will say that is making a comeback soon.

Down the years the honours have come but always in the eye of the storm. There remained a wildness about Lester: champion apprentice at 14 but already into rough-riding suspensions; his first Derby at 18 (on Never Say Die, a month after Roger Bannister broke the four-minute mile) but then six months off for an incident at Royal Ascot. He bitterly resented that verdict, but it was a sort of snarling, competitive resentment that was part of the manic drive that took him to nine Derbys, 11 jockeys' championships and more than 5,000 winners around the globe.

Often you would feel that he was getting his own back on the world, although many times the corners he got into were of his own making. Born an only child with poor hearing and, later, faulty speech, his triumphs would never be of a social kind. But both sides of his family had been champion jockeys, and on horseback he could take them all on.

Right from the beginning there was an extraordinary intuitive talent for riding the thoroughbred. His first Derby mount, in 1951, was on Zuccero, a horse that other jockeys couldn't start. But Piggott also had a violence about him that would go to any lengths to succeed.

Ironically—in view of this week's comeback—part of this drive was a sense of being on borrowed time. He started to waste in his early teens, his 5ft 7in frame naturally at least 2 stone above his 8st 7lb riding weight. His father, Keith, and his grandfather, Ernie, who won three Grand Nationals, were both distinguished national hunt jockeys and Piggott looks back wryly with the words, "I always thought I was going to go jumping."

In February 1957 he stood on the scales at 11st 4lb. At the end of a horrific description of the privations that ensued, he muttered coolly, "I never let it go up again." It was the most ruthless statement of self-denial you ever heard. But it was also a brutal statement of fact, and in later years the scales had been largely conquered: he was no longer a thin man with a fat man trying to get out—witness his trim 8st 10lb today. It has always seemed as if the suppression of physical appetite sharpened the hunger for the two things on which his talents and circumstance could most freely feed: winners and money.

They were inextricably and, finally, criminally entwined. So that while the legend grew of his restless pursuit of mounts in all places, so too did that of his particular idea of the "rate for the job". If the phone went and the lingering silence indicated that Lester was at the other end, his opening welcome line "I'll ride yours next week" would soon be followed by reference to his need to be "looked after".

His special attraction was also the cause of his downfall. He put himself above and beyond the law; above the laws of nature, the laws of racing and finally the laws of the land.

Taking on the first two brought him mass adulation. Even when he transgressed, took somebody else's ride, caused some havoc on the track, there would soon be some other mighty deed—on Nijinsky, The Minstrel, Roberto—and all would be forgiven. There is no one in the racing game who cannot amuse bystanders with a tale of Piggott derring-do, whether it be some astonishing finish with the whips up and the money down, or some inspired piece of cheek such as the "borrowing" of French jockey Alain Lequeux's whip one day at Deauville.

The sad thing about the unequal contest which led to his year's jail sentence for tax evasion in 1987 is both that it need not have happened (he just seemed physically unable to face the need for full disclosure of his earnings), and that beforehand it had really looked as if Lester would climb out on to the sunlit uplands when his riding days were over.

It has been a poignant duty this week to wander back through the cuttings and to remember the degree of serenity about Piggott as he worked towards closing his career at 50. He may be a modest and unpretentious man in conversation but his living-room is a temple to his talent. Paintings and photos of the great man coiled up behind the horse's ears, evoking memories that will never fade.

Watching him sitting there, cigar in one hand, telephone in the other (his deafness never prevented him hearing of a likely winner), and talking about horses and people, you remembered the odd Brando-esque one-liner with which he can surprise you. How long, he had been asked on TV, would he take to set up as a trainer? Pause and then, before the short snuffling laugh, the reply, "About five minutes."

In 1986 that confidence looked justified, 30 winners, including one at Royal Ascot, a training partnership with his wife, Susan, the sheikhs and other top owners on the books.

But then the clouds gathered in, and the torment of what the staff still call his "holiday" was added to by a dreadful riding accident which put Susan into intensive care. After she recovered and he returned, they doggedly put the bits together, but it was slow going: the stable's seasonal total stands at just 11 winners.

So Lester has looked increasingly lost and forlorn, and when this mood was compounded last month by another tabloid attack on his private life, his despair was so deep that some of us quite seriously worried about his sanity.

In those circumstances you can imagine the enthusiasm for a sight of Piggott, however old, marching out once again towards the paddock. So he might not be the rider of yesteryear, so there is the chance of pain and failure ahead; but the last few years have had all that and plenty more. If it makes the man buzz, it will make others buzz too.

The logical view must be that we are on a downward path, but there is a reason for thinking otherwise. This is the centaur theory. Piggott on the track is only the top half of the performance; the real power of the legs and body belong to the horse beneath. What really matters from the man above is equine psychology and judgement of pace. "Lester still knows more about racehorses than anyone else," said one megastar who had better remain nameless as he then added: "A lot of the others only know they are trotting when their caps fall over their eyes."

So the dream still glows and big trainers around the world may yet support it. Bill Shoemaker won the Breeders' Cup Classic at 57, and there is an old hill-billy still going round in West Virginia at 68. For when Lester climbs up behind the mane, it will be on a fresh, and—if his old acquisitive instincts have not deserted him—a talented set of legs. In that sense he will, for those race-spun minutes, be young again.

Every racing fan knows how Lester succeeded beyond the script-writer's wildest dreams. Whatever happens now, he can retire again remembered only as the jockey of jockeys.

One week after writing about Piggott's Breeders' Cup coup on Royal Academy (end of part two), we were facing other reasons for retirement. The brutal imperatives of the jumping game. Even Peter Scudamore has to stare them in the face.

Living on the edge of the pain barrier
November 11th 1990

Is it worth the risk? For 12 tumultuous years Peter Scudamore put every fibre of his being on the line to become the most successful steeplechase jockey in history. Today he has his left leg in plaster, fractured by a horse called Black Humour on Friday. When will the siren sound?

For at 32 Scudamore may have reached the critical moment where he has more to lose than he has to gain. If you go on long enough the ground will always come up to eat you. Scudamore needs no reminding. His Grand National-winning father Michael is lucky to have much face left after that last fall at Wolverhampton. It's a hard game.

Maybe the hardest of them all. Not the most dangerous—in sports like motor racing, mountaineering or hang gliding the risks are mortal every time. But they don't happen day after day, week after week, for an 11-month season. Scudamore had 500 rides last year, and any one of them had the capacity for disaster. Half a ton of horse can capsize on 10 stone of man and the pursuing hoofs are ready to bang like hammers into the jockey's back.

On Friday it was Black Humour at Market Rasen. The horse was favourite, he had won both his races last year, and jumping eight flights of Lincolnshire hurdles shouldn't have been a problem. But the fifth flight was. One false step and Black Humour was rolling in the grass with Scudamore beneath him. As the pack galloped away the jockey got up instinctively, like a boxer from the canvas. But you can't stand for long on a broken leg.

In itself it's not a terrible accident, perhaps three months off, but it's the reminder of the simple brutality of the game that takes even insiders' breath away. A horrible silence fell on the boisterous marquee at Cheltenham when Scudamore's face came up on the television screen and a voice said, "Peter Scudamore's luck has run out at Market Rasen." When it said "a broken leg", there was both a sense of relief and foreboding. It could have been worse. What about next time? Is it worth the risk?

Scudamore's wife, Marilyn, came through quickly. Ten years married, a jockey's sister herself, she was busy that day with Chasing Promotions, the company she runs with her husband. She was shaken—"I'll have a cup of tea just to settle down"—but ready to resume the nursing routine. "It's just such a long old drive to Market Rasen."

There have been other journeys, plenty of them. The leg has been broken before, and the arm, and the wrist, the ribs, the collarbones of course, and worst of all a skull fracture back in 1981. Marilyn has always insisted, quite rightly, that her husband was more at risk on the road than on the racetrack. But she and Peter have young Thomas and Michael at home, and the farm, and all the trophies to admire. Marilyn Scudamore too will have to wonder —how long?

However difficult the decision, Marilyn knows that her partner has thought through his calling more deeply than any jockey before him. "I have never consciously wanted to be anything but a jockey"—the words were spoken at Worcester 11 years ago next month and the memory is still clear of that polite but very direct look, son of a famous racing family yet already very much his own man.

Weighty matters in the Weighing Room? Peter Scudamore (centre) and Graham McCourt in conference (Chris Smith)

"But I don't like comparing myself with other people," he went on. "That way you get yourself confused. I want to compare myself today with myself yesterday, that way you get better." He was 21. There was already composure not bravado. This was the god-fearing, A-Level educated, former deputy head boy of Belmont Abbey School in Herefordshire. His mother had wanted him to be an estate agent. I remember very clearly the impact as he added, quietly, "By next year I want to be the best."

He nearly was. With 91 winners he was clear of the champion John Francome before that skull fracture pulled the curtains on the season. The next year was almost a re-run. Scudamore clear with 120 winners before a bad fall at Southwell put his left arm in limbo. Francome then refused to pass Scudamore's total—one of those instinctive acts of generosity which have always threatened to give John something close to a good name.

It was four years before Francome, the most gifted rider of this or any generation, had left the stage and allowed us to realise that Scudamore was a lot more than the cranked-up obsessive who in 1982 had one admiring fellow rider say, "He has got to change or he will kill himself."

At Newbury on Wednesday Scudamore looked back at that period with the serenity of achievement. "When you are younger you don't believe you are going to get hurt," he said, sitting on the long wooden bench in the jockeys' changing room while some tense, fresh-faced novice riders filed out for the last race.

What's fascinating about him is his directness, and what you might call his sophisticated enthusiasm. After all, he has scaled heights unthought of before his time. His record-breaking 221 winners two seasons ago was a quite unbelievable performance. He is intelligent, he has travelled the world, yet here he was reviewing his motives without a hint of being either conceited or blasé.

"When you are younger," he continued, the pale face glowing at the recollection of the rashness of youth, "you drive cars fast, you drive motorbikes fast. Whenever you are racing you want to be champion jockey. You would ride a rusty bike in the Grand National."

By any standards this is an exceptionally tough man. But he doesn't talk tough. The voice is quiet, serious but above all applied, fascinated by its subject. "There comes a time when you believe you are good enough," he adds, "and you realise you will have to alter to survive. I have probably quietened down a little bit, I have altered my riding technique and with riding better horses you have to build the confidence in yourself that you will have the ability to avoid getting hurt."

When a senior player ruminates about his game, you often begin to wonder if he isn't considering swapping his boots for carpet slippers. But Scudamore has always been like this. Others like Francome, especially like Biddlecombe before him, can be the dashing cavaliers of legend. Scudamore

*Concentration is all.
Peter Scudamore
before the start at
Newbury in
November 1990
(Norman Lomax)*

is serious, has reasoned out an unreasonable game in a way that's never been done before.

The old sweats used to laugh at him. That was all long ago. You can't deny a life force like Peter Scudamore. On Monday at Wolverhampton he notched up his 50th winner of the season, 12 days behind his record schedule, but champions used only to get the half-century up by Christmas. On Tuesday he spoilt every sentimentalist's day by beating Desert Orchid at Devon and Exeter. Here at Newbury he had been out in the paddock early to ride the favourite in the third.

The horse was nervous. It was called New Duds and was trained, like so many of Scudamore's winners, by Martin Pipe, the little limping dynamo from Somerset. Trainer and jockey conferred briefly. Scudamore at 5ft 9in a tall, intense, almost stringy figure. He was legged up into the saddle and set off for the start.

This was only an ordinary hurdle race and New Duds finally weakened to be third. But the cocooned concentration of his jockey was almost tangible from the stands. It is that which has set him apart. The riding style, rather more upright and less athletically blended than that of the challenging Richard Dunwoody, is not the thing. With Scudamore it's the mind. How long will that hold out?

"I get nervous," he says with candour. "But just as nervous on a well-fancied horse as on a bad ride. I also get nervous schooling because so many things can go wrong. I ride better nervous, I am ready for anything."

We were now really into the heart of the "inner game" and sitting there at Newbury on Wednesday you had to marvel at the man. It had been one of those gentle autumn, liquid sunlight days, not many runners, country-clad spectators with talk drifting about farm prices and deer-hunting bans. You could be lured into taking it all as a genial day out. Not Scudamore.

"I was reading the other day about Ayrton Senna," he said, "of how at times he holds his breath while he is driving, to make him more aware. I can understand that. You have to do things to make yourself sharp. When I go to the paddock, I am basically pretty touchy and edgy. I am snappy but I let myself be snappy because I am sharper then. Yesterday at Devon, everyone was going on about Desert Orchid but I felt we could beat him. I was quite wound up."

In recent years the Scudamore mind has been so much one of the wonders of sport that you might not be surprised to learn it also invokes divine intervention. "Down at the start I will always say a 'Hail Mary'," he says. "It's not so much a religious thing, although I am a believer. It's like a chant, a meditation, to make me focus. It's the little things that count. You have to be sharp enough to make them happen."

He is still fascinated by his own experiences. "Take Monday, at Wolver-hampton," he says with a laugh, his voice dropping almost to a whisper because of the confidence he is about to impart. "Two runners in the race, I am about 10-1 on and get left at the start. Everything goes wrong and then at half-way the other horse runs out. That's when you need double, double concentration, a Hail Mary at every fence."

He is warming to his theme but aware of the oddity. "Sometimes I will jump three fences with 'Our Father' and then the next three with 'Hail Mary', it makes you wonder! But what you are trying to do is to get your mind into the horse, leave him alone as much as possible. He has to do the running. It's down to the horse."

Nonetheless this remains a strongly physical and highly dangerous game. On Wednesday you noticed the long scar up the inside of Scudamore's left wrist, and the other wrist still won't flex properly after the injury last April. "But you have got to put negative thoughts out of your mind," he said. "I don't like pain, I hate the dentist, but I don't carry the worry around with me. The hardest thing is seeing somebody else get hurt. They have a crashing fall and you say that could be me."

Now it is him. Again. Scudamore lies in Nottingham Hospital, wondering how soon he can be back in the saddle and many may wonder if he ought to go there at all. It's easy to be cautious from afar and some wise words ring back from the boxing commentator and former world champion Jim Watt. "The trouble for many top sportsmen," said Jim earlier in the week, "is that they fear the rest of their life could be anti-climax."

We had been talking about how boxers, like jump jockeys, face up to the prospect of pain. Beside the caveat that "if you were very worried by pain you would fall by the wayside early on", Jim was very specific. "Pride is the main ingredient," he said. "Pride in yourself, pride in your country, pride in your family. When it gets really rough, and you have got to grit your teeth and put it over the other fellow it's pride that is going to make you do it."

Listening to Scudamore last week there was no doubt that the pride is stronger than ever. "I am more rationalised now," he had said, "but defeat still hurts. Which is good. It grates even more when Richard beats you and you read in the paper that Richard Dunwoody is the best jockey that ever lived. That grates, but it's good to have the fire."

Yet what about the fear of anti-climax, of clinging on too long? "I don't want to go on and get knocked about with scars all over me," Scudamore responded. "And I might give you a different answer in January when we have been trailing round all the tracks and are tired. But at the moment it's exciting. I got up at 6 o'clock this morning to go and school new horses at Charlie Brooks'. I have 200 to ride and each one has a chance of being something. It's a team game and that certainly keeps you going."

Jim Watt had continued: "Nothing I ever do in my life can compare with being champion of the world. But I don't wish I was still doing it. It's too bloody hard. I am having a better time now being a former champion than I ever did as a champion."

"But then in Peter's case," he added thinking across the spectrum, "it sounds as if he dearly loves what he is doing. If he can still do it, he will want to continue. It is giving him something."

At times like that, there is an almost poetic quality about Watt's delivery. He and Scudamore would recognise the truth of that great closing verse from Longfellow:

> "Ask not," the helmsman answered,
> "The secrets of the sea.
> Only those that brave its dangers
> Can comprehend its mystery."

Incredibly, Peter was back in January, leg plated like a Meccano man. The winners picked up again but the questions will remain until the saddle is finally put aside.

Then Scudamore will face other challenges. He may even chance his arm at the training game. It's a harsh business and there is no set pattern for success. Unless, like David Elsworth, you have the gypsy touch.

Broadening horizons for racing's Dr Dolittle
March 3rd 1991

For David Elsworth, Desert Orchid has been the end. The end of the beginning. The end of the time when only those closest to him realised that Dr Dolittle was back. That David Elsworth too could talk to the animals.

Those are fancy words, particularly in the venal, technical, technicolour world of big-time racing where Elsworth is headed. But they are the real explanation. Of Desert Orchid and of all the others.

No one else has ever operated across the top of the training range in the way David Elsworth does today. The early-morning sortie which sees 12-year-old Desert Orchid tuning for Thursday week's Gold Cup showdown at Cheltenham also contains the four-year-old In The Groove, Europe's highest-rated filly on the flat last season.

It's like coaching both a hardened old distance runner and a brilliant young girl sprinter. But more than coaching. Both of them have been with David since the equivalent of primary school. He has made his way as a teacher, a headmaster now. Only his 100 pupils cannot talk.

Not to you and me they can't. But to Elsworth communication is the absolute key. If you have had to work your way up from nothing, or to be exact from an old Commer truck, two borrowed horses, and a first time out double at Newton Abbot 20 years ago next month, you have to know when your athlete is prime.

"They tell you themselves," says Elsworth, the voice still as Wiltshire as the Whitsbury horizon. "Sometimes the signals are very strong. They radiate well-being. The lads will say, 'This is smashing, guvnor. This horse is bopping. He is well.'"

Around him circle 40 head of thoroughbreds. Desert Orchid, white and proud, leads the string as always. Old turf gallops and modern all-weather strips stretch into the distance. A portable phone in the trainer's pocket will soon ring to discuss import regulations for American yearlings. Big deal, but the real language was learnt long ago.

They found him with them in the field when he was eight years old. They were huge, cussed shire horses whom the local farmer had trouble in catching. For David it had been natural. When he got back to the cottage he said simply, "One day I am going to have a stable and horses all around me." The odds must have been a million to one.

He was brought up by his grandparents to farm labourer's expectations. Getting himself a job as a carrot-chopping, muck-shifting stable lad in nearby Collingbourne Ducis was hardly a ticket to stardom. But it took him to horses. Even, for the first time, to ride them.

These stories now tend to drop into a sort of bow-legged Dick Whittington saga. Of how the tiny stable lad becomes the apple of his master's eye and soars to be star apprentice and champion jockey before marrying the trainer's daughter, taking over the whole shooting match, and winning the Derby in his first season. It was not quite like this for David Elsworth.

His first race ride was typical. As old Alec Kilpatrick did his trainer's rounds one evening, he stuck an envelope between the bars of the box where Elsworth was grooming.

"What's that?" asks the boy David. "It's your jockey's licence," says Kilpatrick, who hid a kindly heart behind an austere Scottish countenance. "What for?" queries the unqualified youth. "You ride Go Well tomorrow at Windsor," comes the unexpected answer. "I thought it was Christmas," relates Elsworth. "I rushed over to the lads' hostel to tell them the news. They all hooted at me and said, 'You'll never get round.' I didn't. And as I walked back up the track I remember Lester Piggott looking over the rails. He was all sun-tanned from his winter holidays. He was with 'Teasy Weasy' Raymond. They were roaring with laughter."

The recollection is vivid but it doesn't have any rancour. Whatever fuelled Elsworth it was not envy. "I rode my first winner the next year at Cheltenham when I was only 17—Rathronan at 100-8, a chestnut horse with a white face. The trouble was it took me two years to ride the next one. I was like many jockeys. In the right place I could have been a 20-winners-a-year man, and by the end I knew what I was doing. Anyway, it was all good experience.''

This, of course, is the wisdom of hindsight. At the time few even in the racing pond would have noticed as David paddled from Alec Kilpatrick, to Fulke Walwyn, to Doug Marks and on. But over those 15 years the Elsworth eyes were opened and the understanding of the creatures on whom the whole game depends became more acute.

It was a random, hotch-potch education. The only real mentor seems to have been Jim Templeman, the Head Lad at Kilpatrick's. "He was a great feeder, wonderful around the stable," says Elsworth. "I used to sit with him. He really knew his horses."

In many ways it was a *metier* that was learned by default. Elsworth was bumping round the bottom rung of the jumping ladder. The realisation came to him that he could do the job a lot better than most of the people he rode for.

"There was one old guy who used to hate to take his horses out in the rain and get the tack dirty," he remembers. "When I was down there he kept saying, 'Don't give them another canter, boy. Them will be worn out.' But I managed to persuade him to let me do as I wanted.

"He had this animal that had kept on falling. When I went to ride it at Wincanton one of the jockeys came up and said, 'Watch out, that is lethal.' In the race the horse seemed fine until I got knocked off him at the ditch. Everybody said, 'There you are,' and said it again when he got brought down at Newbury. But then he won his next two easily and I realised that he had only been falling because he wasn't fit."

That experience may have reinforced Elsworth's self-belief but, already turning 30, he was not likely to attract clients eager to back him on a training career. Cue for the tale of Indulgent and Willoblige, landers of the famous double at Newton Abbot and the first horses fully conditioned by Elsworth albeit under the name of Colonel Ricky Vallance at Bishops Canning.

David rode them himself. The bets were placed, especially on the second horse Willoblige. Afterwards his little band of supporters shared out the money in a pub in Bournemouth. "I was the most understanding, tolerant person that god had ever created."

The word was out.. Elsworth understood how to deliver. Other punters were drawn to the flame. Eighteen months later, still under Ricky Vallance's name, he had attracted some 20 horses to Bishops Canning and one of them, Red Candle, had landed a major coup when beating Red Rum in the Hennessy Gold Cup at Newbury.

But it was too good to last. The next spring the Vallance stable was

A man and his mission. David Elsworth on the gallops at Whitsbury (Adam Scott)

warned off over the running of a horse called Well Briefed. "The truth is they didn't like the Colonel not being in charge," says Elsworth. "I had done nothing wrong with the horse, but they didn't believe it. Talk about the vegetarian fox being caught in the chicken run."

It was six long years before David got together the backing to start out for real as a trainer. Six years doing odd jobs: working a clothes stall at Romsey market, running a livery yard on Salisbury Plain.

He was 39. It wasn't much better than a cattle stable but he had waited a long time. He didn't hang about. Fortune Cookie opened the account on March 23rd 1979 in a hurdle race at Devon and Exeter. Within a month David had landed six more winners including a double on the flat at Epsom. The "shrewdies" began to notice. Any horse, any distance, Elsworth might know the score.

In the racing game we soon became accustomed to this rollicking, restless West Countryman who was always likely to upset your calculations. But in the last three years Elsworth has gone out to a much wider audience. In 1988 he won the Grand National with Rhyme 'N' Reason and the next year mixed Royal Ascot's premier sprint, the Kings Stand Stakes, with Desert Orchid's epic Gold Cup at Cheltenham.

Ah, Desert Orchid! There he is at the head of the string. Because of television and his own, grey-ghost, front-running style, he is now the most popular horse in history. Out here at Whitsbury, the Roman camp on the high uplands five miles south of Salisbury, he is their own personal living legend. But he is also a racehorse they have to get ready to run.

Elsworth has been intoning the litany of horses' names as they file past the jeep. "That's a nice three-year-old by Palace Music that has never run . . . that's Jaffa Line, she won the Candelabra at Goodwood . . . that's Mighty Falcon, a full brother to Mighty Fly . . . that's . . ." He breaks off for a second to concentrate on the old grey up front, once again favourite for the Gold Cup on Thursday week.

"We will have to get him to Cheltenham really smack on," says David, "and he will be the one the others have to beat. But he is not as good round there, round to the left. There's no reason to it but he doesn't get his rhythm. If you were sailing you would say there was no wind in his sails."

A bottle of Calvados had taken a terrible hammering the previous night but there was nothing wrong with Elsworth's alertness or with his untutored eloquence. "I am not going to get any more thrills from Desert Orchid," says his trainer. "He has done everything. I would like to stop him after Cheltenham, then bring him up earlier next summer to try and get ready for the King George."

"The trouble is," he adds, warming to the "Is Dessie finished?" debate which will become inflamed again next week, "it gets increasingly difficult to get him fit. It's like cooking. You can't just turn the heat up or you have burnt the outside with the inside still not done. The horse hasn't really sent us any very strong signals since last February and I don't think he will again."

Suddenly amid all the rural bustle of the training routine, lads joshing, horses stomping, long dogs running beside the wagon, you get hit again by the realisation that the ambitions now stretch way beyond Desert Orchid. Behind a carefree and sometimes impetuous exterior (don't try and carve him up in a motor car) there is a driving urge to top the lot.

Elsworth puts his head forward when he makes a point as if he's testing the wind for reaction. "I have got some good runners for Cheltenham [make a note of Riverhead, Floyd and Major Inquiry] but I am not sure I like jumping as much as I did. It's hard on the horses. If you run a colt a mile and a half on the flat he's had a good blow but he's not knackered. You see an old chaser coming in after running three miles with 12 stone you feel a bit sorry for him. Mind you it takes a real man to do it."

We are back to talking of, and to, the animals. Sensitive but not sentimental: "That's a nice colt by Woodman . . . that's a nice filly, she worries a bit but she's got an engine . . ." The belief is in fitness of mind as well as body. "The one pitfall is when you have a horse very fit and well and you think 'Christ, he has never been better,' but he runs too free and stops effing dead. He is over the top, over-trained. That is the only thing that catches us out. Other than that they tell you most times."

There is a stockman's confidence in what he has done. Yet now he is pitching these skills into an altogether bigger market, the multi-million dollar flat racing game where the rewards are huge but the pressures are greater. If their connections will excuse the metaphor, the successes of both Desert Orchid and In The Groove have been cases of silk purses from the sows' ears. Now the ears are from a classier kind.

The expectations are greater and only time will tell whether Elsworth's flair can still triumph at this highest level. The three long-suffering linchpins to his life, his wife Jane, the secretary Chris Hill, and Head Lad Rodney Boult, will be needed more than ever. In his own way David seems to recognise this.

"Now Rodney, he's a top man," says the trainer. "We go back years. I used to drive him down here from Doug Marks'. I had a Heinkel bubble car, URX 512, petrol was 5/11 a gallon. But he's too nice to the staff. Luckily I cut up a bit noisy, and scream and shout so it balances out. You have got to show you care."

He realises that there is an image of a vassal-kicking tyrant and adds: "I tell you something. They believe in what we are doing. If you asked them where they would send a top horse if they owned it, they would all say here. We were fifth on the flat last year. The Aga has taken his horses away from Stoute and Cumani, Sangster is cutting down. We might have a chance."

In The Groove trots by, still woolly from her winter break. "She's only cantering but I want to get her ticking over. She has so much class, and if you can switch her off, she just pootles along and pootles along, and when you pick her up she goes." There is talk of the top prizes in Europe. Even if the Prix Ganay is still pronounced "Garnay" we have certainly travelled a long way from selling hurdles at Taunton.

An owner comes over the hill. It is Alan Argeband, noted West Country clothier, tennis player and seeker after good things for tomorrow's card. He has seen it all from the beginning. He even provided the cloth in the bad days on the markets.

"I love him," said Alan, looking across to where Elsworth is standing with some two-year-olds. "He drinks too much. He's no businessman. He's always buying horses without having owners for them. But he's a genius.

"Take my filly, Miss Simplicity. She won last year in September, although everybody hated her because she kept whipping round. He just says, 'She's a cracker. Look at her, she's smiling at us.' I tell you they are his pals."

4. Horses to Hitch a Wagon To

Officially they all trace back to those first three founding fathers from Araby. But this collection of thoroughbreds is about as polyglot as a UNICEF meeting. What they have in common is not just running ability but the special charisma that makes men want to hitch their wagons up behind them.

Some pretty colourful humans also get caught up in the baggage train. Try these characters up from under to support the Australian champion Strawberry Road in the Arc of 1984.

Out of the blue comes a kangaroo
October 7th 1984

Whose blood on the kangaroo's glove? Incredibly, after one of the worst weeks for self-inflicted wounds in Australian history, it may not be Aussie's own. Come this evening, their horse Strawberry Road may have won the Arc de Triomphe, banished scandal from every front page back home and blown the racing world wide open.

Not for nothing does Strawberry Road carry the boxing-kangaroo symbol made famous by Alan Bond's victorious yachting mission to the America's Cup last summer. When this five-year-old Australian champion joins his 21 rivals at the start line at Longchamp this afternoon, he will have travelled as far as any nautical adventurer.

He'll be facing an equally historic and unprecedented task, and for back-up in the long months of foreign preparation he has relied not on squads of heavyweight supporters, but on a small if jaw-jutting crew of one—his young trainer John Nicholls, who has gambled his whole career in pitching "Strawberry" against the best in the world.

You wouldn't have found too many believers back on June 1, when the 34-year-old Nicholls led Strawberry Road wearily into his new French home at Lamorlaye on the edge of the forest 25 miles north of Paris at the end of 27 flying hours from Sydney via California.

"No, there wasn't much of a reception party," John admitted cryptically last week. "And for the first few days they thought I was completely mad. I had this paranoia about him getting European flu. I scrubbed the whole box from top to toe. I brought my own feed bucket, and knocked the wire grill from the top of his door so he could hang his head outside. People were very kind, but you could see that they thought we were hicksville."

Overleaf: The 1987 Derby (Chris Smith) Patrick Biancone has been the suave, smiling youthful bulk under whose wing Strawberry Road and Nicholls were placed. He also is a third-

Holding a star. Brough Scott with Strawberry Road at Chantilly (Chris Smith)

generation trainer, and he saddles last year's winner, All Along, the impressive Sagace and Castle Guard this afternoon.

Biancone likes to pull success out of a conversation like a conjurer's rabbit: "I say your only chance to win a Group One in Europe is the Grand Prix at Baden-Baden. Presto, the first Australian horse to do it in history!" But even Patrick admits to being shaken by the performance of both the horse and man in Germany.

Not only did Strawberry Road first run a close second in his warm-up race over one mile before beating Esprit du Nord in the Grand Prix, but John Nicholls did his usual double stint of being both trainer and stable lad with an arm so badly infected it had to be strapped useless to his side.

After that victory, people at Chantilly and beyond began to realise the qualities which had brought Strawberry Road victory in 13 of his 26 races, culminating in a brilliant triumph last October in the one-and-a-quarter mile Cox Plate, the most prestigious weight-for-age race in Australia.

Back at Lamorlaye, they also realised the relentless determination of a young man who in three-and-a-half months has never missed a day with his horse, and who brought six cases of extra vitamins and additives with him. The respect with which the vet helped to administer a glucose intravenous drip on Tuesday morning was testimony to the way in which Nicholls has won them over.

Yet if John is a professional, so too is the horse who was first dispatched to Queensland from his New South Wales birthplace because the training was cheaper, and was then dismissed by top jockey Mick Dittman as "a mangy little mongrel". Still not more than 15.3 hands, but long and muscular, Strawberry Road, with his distinctive yellow bridle, has a hard and purposeful look. He has also been noticeable in the separate mile-and-a-quarter work-outs he has done with both Sagace and All Along in the last 10 days, each time finishing alongside them.

Patrick Biancone watched the three horses walking round in the chilly damp of Chantilly Forest on Tuesday: "Strawberry Road—I do not think he is really top class. But I tell you one thing, he is very tough. This year's Arc will be a tough race, so maybe he 'as a good chance. A surprise, eh?"

It certainly won't be a surprise for the two cheery great antipodean hulks

Tie him down, sport? John Nicholls and Australian hope Strawberry Road, ready for the Arc de Triomphe (Chris Smith)

who greeted us on return to the yard. Part-owners Ray Steer and John Singleton have each had A$1,000 on the nose at 100-1.

From his chest-pocket, Steer keeps producing a snapshot of Strawberry Road when he won the AJC Derby, with Sydney mud up to the hocks, by nine lengths from Singleton's horse, Valeso. Singleton is a sort of ocker version of Terry Wogan, and eventually bought his half-share from the colt's original Greek owners last April with the magnificent gesture of writing ''IOU a million dollars'' on a used betting slip.

Singleton and Steer also have studs, and are well aware that victory in the Arc has much financial significance for their horse, and for Australian racing as a whole. Strawberry Road's value will increase some 20 times if he wins today. But, having travelled across the world just to see him run, having commandeered an Australian flag to wave across Longchamp, they are unlikely to lose their sense of the absurd.

Earlier this year, rumours were sweeping Australia that the big-spending Maktoum family would attend the Sydney yearling sales. Singleton hired two Middle Eastern gentlemen and made them pay A$20 a throw for a round of drinks. The racing circle nearly collapsed in the rush.

If Strawberry Road slugs his rivals out of it today, Singleton won't need a limmo. He'll be on cloud nine until the snow falls in Sydney.

Strawberry Road didn't last home at Longchamp but he ran in practically every other major event short of the Boat Race and finished a fast closing second to Pebbles in the Breeders' Cup.

Big shots, grand places, that's where the media spotlight tends to focus. So as the dust settled at the end of 1984 it was worth taking time out at the other end of the scale. Not the best but the busiest, a horse called Carriage Way.

The Nijinsky of Middleham
October 28th 1984

It's prizegiving time again. The literary world may still be agape at the 33-1 turn-up in the Booker Prize, but that will be as nothing if I have my way in the Horse of the Year awards for which voting starts next week. Naturally there are already some impressive candidates to argue over. Teenoso, hero of the magnificent King George at Ascot in July; Chief Singer, the explosive ex-invalid who played in the highest class over three different distances; Provideo, whose astonishing 15 victories set a twentieth-century record for a two-year-old; and El Gran Senor, whose Two Thousand Guineas defeat of Chief Singer was the individual performance of the season.

These claims notwithstanding, our nomination voyage on Wednesday took us not to Newmarket or to wherever poor El Gran Senor's tootsies are being treated, but to rain-lashed Middleham in North Yorkshire, whose greatest claim nowadays is that old Richard III haunts the castle.

For if the game needs stars, it also needs roots, and our vote goes to a nearly black horse whose career has put him right into the bedrock of it all. Admittedly, in a race, Carriage Way needs a furlong start from any of those principals, and in terms of fame he has as much chance of making the front cover of *Pacemaker* as the Pope of going centre-fold in *Playboy*.

But then Carriage Way has been battling since before the others were even a gleam in a stallion's eye, and yet at 10 years old he has now put together a season of no fewer than 27 appearances, which is twice the totals of the English (Secreto), Irish (El Gran Senor), and French (Darshaan) Derby winners combined.

As Carriage Way's activities have also stretched to getting a mare in foal the day after winning the 8.45p.m. race at Hamilton on July 18th, many of our credits have been confined to giggles about "Mr Versatility". In fact, despite five mares in 1983, the post-Hamilton jaunt was his only coupling this season—no surprise considering that in seven months he carried nine different jockeys on 16 separate courses as far apart as Ayr, Sandown, Yarmouth, and Chepstow. What's more, he ended it not as some played-out old hat-rack, but in glorious televised triumph two Saturdays ago, the £6,000 *Daily Mirror* Apprentice Final, at York, the biggest win of his career.

Carriage Way's three other successes this term give him overall figures of 17 victories and over £60,000 from 18 outings in nine full seasons since he originally joined Ryan Price in Sussex from his Cotswold birthplace on Arthur Smith's farm at Sopworth. Ownership soon passed to a Soho porn magnate, Dave Sullivan; for a season his training switched to Neville Callaghan at Newmarket; and then, at Doncaster, in October 1979, "Carrie" was knocked down for just 3,500 guineas to the small, squat, shrewd-looking figure of his present trainer, Bill Stubbs.

A half-share was immediately sold to Ray Reynold, a Middlesbrough hotelier, to help finance things as Bill Stubbs and his wife struggled and scraped to keep their handful of horses together. "I bought him because he was the best looker I'd ever seen," says Bill, before adding darkly, "and to prove someone wrong." The 37-year-old Stubbs began as a Darlington stable lad, lost a lung and his racing interest in a dreadful fall at Cheltenham, and now inhabits the bottom end of the racing ladder where the owners are small, the horses slow, and the rungs slippery.

"The art of training," he says abruptly, playing his fingers on Carriage Way's hard old neck, "is to get them fit, to know when they are right, and to place them properly."

The old horse looks across attentively, those black legs still as clean as something 10 years younger. "A lot of men wouldn't train Carrie," says Bill Stubbs. "They wouldn't realise how much work he has to have, and you can't put a jockey on him. Dave Nicholls rode him one day, and Carrie just laughed at him. If you have a good apprentice, an uphill finish and soft ground, and you have him right, you can have a bet. I told everybody he was a certainty at York, and in he came at 10-1. We'll win it next year, too."

Next season's plans at the old greystone Tupgill Stables, to which the pair move this January, include an expanded 30-strong team and an enterprising £500 all-in multiple ownership scheme called Nationwide Racing. But first Carriage Way is going to have a full shot at the matrimonials at the Queenstown stud near Enfield. "He is keen enough. Watch this," said Bill Stubbs, and, threading the rein through the bit stallion-style, led the horse out into the courtyard.

Carriage Way immediately began hollering like some equine Tarzan who thinks Jane is just a couple of trees away. Stubbs took his horse hastily back inside, and as they shared the joke, said very privately: "However you get on at stud or on the track next season, I'll never let you go. Never, ever."

A month later another horse, another place and a rather different set of problems. The Japanese have applied themselves to racing with a relentless thoroughness that makes you shake your head in wonder.

The facilities and service are a different class to anywhere else on the globe. But there are still a few things to straighten out on the equine side. Culture shock can happen on four legs too.

Tokyo wakes up to Bedtime
November 25th 1984

Translation is apt to be tricky in Tokyo. At the wedding hotel here on Friday, the lift carried the sign "Bride and Broom Only". What are they going to make of a horse called Bedtime?

By four o'clock this afternoon, seven in the morning your time, the answer could be historic. For if Bedtime wins today's fourth running of the Japan Cup, he'll be scoring the farthest-flung success ever registered by an English-trained horse. More than that, he will change the face of Japanese racing.

Well, to be specific, it's the undercarriage he will be altering. For Bedtime, unlike any of the home runners on the 12-race card, is a gelding, and victory for him could break one of the rigid prejudices which presently blocks a general Japanese improvement.

It would also surely crack the ridiculous ban in Europe on geldings running in Group One races. But although, as a newly found father of four, I am uniquely equipped to advise on the merits of the Bedtime operation, the real joy here has been to watch both locals and visitors trying to come to terms with Lord Halifax's flyer as a future champion.

For even the respectful "Ah-so" politeness has been stretched to the limit these last few mornings, when the Japanese are asked to believe that this enormous, plodding chestnut thing is Britain's best shot for an event immodestly titled The World Thoroughbred Championship. Compared with the shiny, tiptoeing flat-racing elite from eight other nations, Bedtime's great 17-hand, common-headed frame looks as if it has been misrouted from a hurdle race at Newbury. Didn't Willie Carson make a hunting-horn toot through his teeth as he and Bedtime were led on to the track on Thursday?

Oriental bafflement then reached a new pitch as Bedtime breezed for a mile, clocking out the last six furlongs in 1min 10.4sec, the last three in 34.4 and the final furlong in 11.6. The six-furlong time was only 0.3 off the race record at that distance, making this the most astonishing work-out ever seen in Tokyo.

This gallop, and the genuinely bullish air of the foreign entries brought an extra spice to the beflagged pre-race press conference. For against the invasion, the Japanese are this year fielding the two real aces from their pack, last season's triple crown winner, Mr CB, and the unbeaten Symboli Rudolf, who has achieved a similar feat this term. If these two can't stop the raiders making it four cups out of four then, say the Jeremiahs, all is lost for Nippon racing.

Judgement on that after the race. But from what one could squeeze through the language divide beforehand, it didn't seem that the home team had come to town as amateurs.

Sure, the visitors looked good, Esprit du Nord from France, Majesty's Prince and Win from America, Kiwi from New Zealand (where else?) and from Australia both Bounty Hawk and our old friend Strawberry Road, who must now have done more miles than Marco Polo. But on Friday we were also taken to another barn where Symboli Rudolf had just been shipped in, and the awed hush from the local hacks as owner Tomohiro Wada came out to greet us showed that not everyone was a pessimist.

Anyway, that was our untranslated view. What we got from Mr Wada was quite another matter. Wada is a short, square, slow-moving man in his sixties, with a raincoat, a porkpie hat and a smile somewhere in next week.

He is a famous Japanese horse-breeder, and he owned Speed Symboli (Symboli Rudolf's grandsire) their best horse to run overseas. Everything suggests that Mr Wada is a competitor—except for what he said. Or what we were told he said.

Mr Wada (or the interpreter) said that both Mr CB and Symboli Rudolf were very good horses. He didn't think there was a lot between them, but of course they couldn't be anything like as strong as the European animals, and after our long journey he thought it only right that we should take off the prize.

Symboli Rudolf stamped testily on the rice straw beside us. Mr Wada's smile moved a little closer—to about Monday afternoon. We remembered last year and how close the crippled local Keio Promise got to Stanerra, the winner. We didn't believe a word of what Mr Wada said.

But then the Japanese are not alone with inscrutability. After his work-out on Strawberry Road on Friday, the world's greatest jockey was giving what—with the interpreter extending every mutter into a minute's worth —must have been his longest ever press conference. Eventually one excessively polite journalist asked how Lester Piggott kept so strong at his advanced age. Our famous purveyor of false information did not disappoint: "It's all those hormones I keep taking," Lester said on the volley. Ah-so! They are translating it still.

Bedtime ran a gallant second to Symboli Rudolf, the best Japanese horse I have seen in eight trips to Tokyo. There is a bit of talk of trace-clipping and castration but it may take a while yet.

Not too long a delay for a big British win abroad. Forgive the hiccups in this report from Chicago the following August, but you will understand we had something to celebrate.

He made Chicago our kind of town
September 1st 1985

There's nothing better in racing than the moment you know you have it beat. That's what it was like when Teleprompter came off the turn on Sunday.

Sure, the winning ticket was burning a hole in my pocket. True, we visiting Brits were on to a hiding if one of our much trumpeted invaders couldn't put it across the American defence last week. But as Teleprompter changed his legs and quickened clear of his pursuers, nothing could touch us.

This was the greatest overseas success for the noble house of Derby ("The 16th Earl?" asked the TV interviewer; "18th, actually," answered his lordship). It was the finest performance yet in Bill Watts' gifted training career. It was pure "punch in the air" joy for jockey Tony Ives (so much so that he overpunched at the finish and damn near fell off). But above all it was a triumph for Teleprompter, the horse as hero.

For despite carrying the famous white cap and black jacket of the Derby silks, Teleprompter has been something of an outsider to top British flat-racing circles. He hails from the now unfashionable North. He began his journey in such unclassic haunts as Carlisle and Redcar. And anyway, as a gelding, he is peculiarly unqualified for the international payola of the breeding game.

Yet long before he had gone out to do his two minutes' worth of business on the track last week, it was clear that Teleprompter had a character to match his achievements. A tall, raking, honest-headed bay, he looks so much more the sort you would find walking round before the Champion Hurdle in March than the Derby in June that one American scribe called him the ugliest horse he had ever seen. But just because he has been around a bit, and maybe even because racing is the only thing on the horizon, Teleprompter has a marvellous gentle big man's self-possession. "Look at him," said Watts as we stood in the horse's box before racing, "you could have the kids in here with him."

How did this paragon, this richest single winner Britain has ever produced, emerge from the chrysalis of the great raw-boned "boat" which Willy Carson could only get home tenth of 14 in his first race at Doncaster three years ago? "To be honest," said Bill Watts, repeating treasured lines, "I always thought a bit of him as a two-year-old, but he just lost his rhythm that first time and couldn't run again because of a virus. So he was cut [gelded] in the winter and we set out to win some handicaps as a three-year-old. He didn't do too badly, winning the Britannia at Royal Ascot and beaten a short head in the Cambridgeshire."

It was a good campaign, but it still only brought a Timeform rating of 104 compared to the 122 after 1984's big race successes in England, France and Ireland, and some 130-odd today. Obviously the big frame has made continued physical improvement, but Watts cites two other reasons for Teleprompter's progress: the fitting of blinkers in 1984—Teleprompter used to roll and hang under pressure—and refining them to a visor (blinkers with a back window) this season. "After Ascot last year, Willie said that he did not fight back until he could see Katies in front of him. With a visor he sees them coming."

It is this feeling that the animal would go out and fight till he drops—the American media called him "The Rambo horse"—which has captured the imagination of the public, but it has touched those closest to him even more deeply. As Jimmy Swales and Ginger Caine led Teleprompter back through the barns after the long and faintly embarrassing formalities of the dope test on Sunday a passing van stopped and two smiling faces and very black locals said, "Is that the Limey horse that won The Million?" and on realising that this was indeed himself they went whooping off in wonderment as Ginger muttered, "You can tell the lads at home that Catterick will never be the same."

All this warmth can be generated only if the horse has scored in the white heat of the race itself, if those around it have planned with the coolness of wisdom, and if the whole enterprise has been blessed with a necessary sprinkle of luck. So it was on Sunday when all Watts's preparation and Teleprompter's power were almost wasted as the race began.

Drawn on the inside rail, Teleprompter missed his kick in the stalls and so the Budweiser Million field was on its way with our hero seeming certain to be cut off on the inside and then be trapped in the pack. Outside Tony Ives was the great Bill Shoemaker, who hasn't won a record 8,000 races by allowing people up his inner. But as Tony screamed for room The Shoe held the door ajar, Ives desperately galvanised Teleprompter up to the lead, and the game had escaped the rest of them.

Back in Richmond, the ancient North Yorkshire town set above the River Swale and below the moors on which Teleprompter is trained, the whole thing is already into well-watered legend. They had had the telegrams, the banners, the mayor, the homecoming and, even if it's hardly worth saying, the final proof that to bar the European public from watching geldings like Teleprompter run in top Group One races is simple nonsense.

Maybe things go even higher than that. For at the end of festivities on Friday, Bill Watts gave one of his long reflective chuckles, looked over Wensleydale, and said: "You know, this horse has been absolutely amazing. For all the trouble, the people, the cameras, he hasn't turned a hair. Animals like him are bred in heaven."

In the eighties it was normally British horses that did the travelling. But the Grand National has always been a law unto itself. In 1986 it drew one of the most intrepid challengers of all.

The Grand National adventure story starts here
March 30th 1986

Of course there will always be love and music and dance, but when you get to Aintree there's another international language. It's written all over the impossible Czech tilt at next Saturday's Grand National. It's simple, glorious, tangible . . . adventure.

That's not to decry the excellent English spoken by Dr Jaroslav Vesely, the group's interpreter. Nor to translate exactly the Slovak wording on the side of their horsebox in which four men, one horse and one Skoda car drove the marathon haul from Moravia a week ago. But spend some time around the trainer-rider Vaclav Chaloupka and his bold, front-running black stallion with the unSlovak name of Essex, and adventure's clearly the game.

It's certainly not prudence. Neither horse nor jockey has been in a race since falling in the Czech version of the Grand National, the Pardubicie, back on October 6th. And the 37-year-old Chaloupka, who originally retired from race-riding four years ago, also admitted: "On his own, Essex would jump the fences, no problem. But with so many others, it may be difficult. I must get hold of him and say, 'Be careful, man'."

Such talk in the comfortable Liverpool seaside suburb of Blundellsands on Tuesday didn't dispel the thought that this intrepid band, complete with identical light grey shoes and dark grey three-piece suits, might be on something of a "jolly", an equestrian equivalent of those "rent-a-bum" heavyweights who come over for a free trip and a quick lie-down.

Those thoughts perished quickly in the Aintree chill next morning. Unfamiliar, unraced and unfancied Vaclav and Essex may be, but when it comes to commitment they belong deep in that main artery of obsession that only dreams of the National can drive.

Let's start with the horse, a big, 16-hand, cosmopolitan eight-year-old with a Russian dam and a Venezuelan sire now stabled in the very box from which Jay Trump and Anglo went out to triumph in '65 and '66. Essex has scars enough to suggest the individuality which made him refuse to enter the starting stalls as a two-year-old in Hungary, and led to his joining Vaclav's 48-strong stable on the Slusovice Cooperative Farm for the un-princely equivalent of £500.

As well as a travel scrape on the near-fore knee and a knarled old tendon from a breakdown on the same leg two seasons ago, Essex also sports a Hungarian racing brand on his wither and a huge mark on his quarters that looks like an amateurish attempt at imprinting the hammer-and-sickle motif. Apparently this was really caused by a nail in a temporary stable, but neither that nor the explanation that his prancing masculinity would not be a problem in the National parade because "he is a sportsman, and so he does not think of girls", allayed fears that Essex might be rather too eccentric.

But then you touch him. Essex may not have run for six months, and he may stamp and snap at the end of his chain as his groom Jerry Paltlak gives him the old-fashioned curry-comb scrape and all-over, but the muscles beneath that gleaming black skin are as hard as rock. Run your fingers down the side of his arched and shiny neck, press your hand back along his ribs and stomach, and you find not just the sinewy firmness of the runner,

but the granite conditioning of the prizefighter. Whatever he's been up to these last few months, no horse will strip readier next Saturday.

Neither will any jockey. Sometimes when a rider takes his shirt off, the impression is of stringy leanness and lumpy collarbones. But when old Vaclav pulls up his vest in the weighing-room on Saturday, some of his rivals will glance in apprehension. Of course, nothing matches the practice of race-riding, but if any man can get primed without it, he must surely be Vaclav Chaloupka.

On Wednesday morning, when we came out of the box prepared to pass on inane compliments to the handler, he was already a sweat-suited speck on the skyline. Half-an-hour later he was back to do a series of gut-wrenching calisthenics, and end it all with a party-piece of diving over the four-foot running rail and an incredible series of forward and backward somersaults. If Essex does turn over next Saturday, you can bet Vaclav will be back on board before he rises.

Czech mates. The Czechoslovak horse Essex and his entourage at Aintree. The car also travelled inside (Chris Smith)

Yet that work-out, and the hour in which Essex trotted and cantered on the course to the beehive-buzz accompaniment of the Aintree preparations, was just a warm-up. For the Czechs, the serious stuff comes in the afternoon. For Essex, two six-furlong spins only 30 seconds apart "for super-compensation", explains Vaclav. And for the trainer-rider-box-driver-blacksmith, a 12-mile run in a 50lb padded jacket.

Chaloupka has an enormous dimple in his chin which points very directly at you when he gets animated. "This winter we have deep-freeze," he says through Dr Vesely, who is also deputy director of Slusovice Farm livestock division. "So we have to work him in the forest. But now he is ready, I will respect him. All my life [he rode his first winner when he was 12] I dream of winning the Pardubicie. I do that four times. Also I dream of Grand National. Now I am waiting for the start."

The 4½-mile Pardubicie is run at a slower tempo than the 4½-mile Liverpool challenge, but its fences include the dreaded "Taxis" (considerably higher than anything here), and Essex had already cleared that and was 300 metres clear when he tripped up at a little fence near the end. "In Czechoslovakia," says Vaclav, "if Essex start, others no chance."

Maybe it will be impossible for Essex on Saturday, but forget easy phrases about "bouncing Czechs" and "Iron Curtain rollers". For this, as Aintree adventures go, is the real thing.

Essex certainly came out fighting. He gave the first three fences about a foot of clearance and it was soon evident that old Vaclav would need every ounce of his muscles to apply the brakes. In fact he put on so much pressure that one of his leathers broke at Bechers and he completed a circuit virtually bare back before he pulled up.

They may not stand on ceremony in Czechoslovakia and they also don't believe in unnecessary frills in Australia. Or they certainly didn't when we were granted an audience with the king of their herd. It was a long way from the glamour of the Breeders' Cup at Santa Anita where we had been four days before.

A little horse to warm Dame Edna's heart
November 9th 1986

We were promised the best horse in the world. No, not Dancing Brave, poor old thing—that was last week in California. This was Wednesday and it was Melbourne, and to see this particular paragon of the four-legged race we had to travel to the seaside suburbs. Bonecrusher lives next to Dame Edna.

To be fair, the pride of Australasia was only lodging at No. 4, Al Benca Street. The fabled Dame Edna's abode must be a little more swish than the Mentone area's usual bungalow and front-garage style. But be certain, few of La Everage's entrances have matched the impact of Bonecrusher's appearance on Wednesday.

For Bonecrusher is a genuine equine superstar, a horse who has won seven Group One races, already netted A$1.5m (£675,000) and who flies to Tokyo this weekend to tilt for another million and immortality as the first southern hemisphere animal to win the Japan Cup. With that on the sheet you have to expect a degree of fanfare and trumpets and some pretty intensive security. At Santa Anita, for instance, Dancing Brave had two huge armed guards who answered the nervous enquiry about whether they had ever . . . er . . . killed someone, with a curl of the lip and a laconic "Yup".

To confound such grand assumptions, Bonecrusher came on last week with all the fuss and fanfare of an empty supermarket trolley. And a pompous Pom like me can do no better than admit "handsome is as handsome does" as this plain, scarred little chestnut was paraded before us.

Well, "paraded" is a rather grand word. Bonecrusher just sloped in past the wiremesh gate, deposited two droppings at our feet, and then cropped a patch of grass in this tiny yard which, since it has already housed Australia's superstar sprinter Manikato, must be the most unlikely home of the famous since Red Rum first clattered out from behind McCain's Car Sales into the centre of Southport.

Old "Rummie" would have looked positively dandyish beside Bone-crusher. There's no proud crest to this horse's neck, no one's done anything fancy to his mane and tail, and while his skin is shiny and supple, it is spread tight enough around his barely 16-hand frame to leave no doubt that this is a *worker*. Right on cue, trainer Frank Ritchie bade us a polite goodbye and led his gelding off for an hour's slog around Mentone, his third outing of the day.

It all seemed a million miles from the palatial yards and polished promenades of our champions in Europe. It was also a far, far cry from the green and white awnings and precision monitoring with which Wayne Lukas trimmed his Breeders' Cup Lady's Secret in America. But final truth in racing always comes from the form book. When you read that by the spring of his four-year-old season, Bonecrusher had already won 13 of his 24 races and remained unbeaten in nine starts at 1½ miles and beyond, you know that his connections don't need any second guessing from the other end of the world.

Watching the horse and listening to Ritchie and owner Peter Mitchell

The pride of Australasia. Bonecrusher with his trainer, Frank Ritchie (left), and owner, Peter Mitchell, looks out for challengers (Tim Hannan)

(35 years ago they were classmates in primary school), Bonecrusher and his team emerge as a marvellous metaphor from New Zealand sporting life. Bonecrusher's connections must have been the sort of kids who would wander to the wicket with one pad, no gloves and a borrowed bat, but then lambast the bowling to every end of the county. The only thing flash about them was the score.

Of humble origins and heavily scarred across the chest from cartwheeling over a wire fence at his Wyatomo birthplace, Bonecrusher raised a mere NZ\$3,250 (£1,152) as a yearling at the Trentham Sales in North Island, New Zealand. With those disadvantages, Ritchie didn't fancy allowing his little colt to indulge in any saucy thinking, and so he promptly had him castrated. Many an English trainer will envy the ease with which everyone Down Under accepts such an operation.

Bonecrusher's first race victory, at his second attempt, was on October 26th, 1984, over just 840 metres at the Ellerslie racecourse, where he is trained near Auckland. He and his team have travelled a long way since then but have not altered either their style, or their belief in themselves. Gary Stewart may not get many other rides, but it was he who was on board that first day in New Zealand and he who has been in the saddle while Bonecrusher has set Australia alight this year. Their final victory —over fellow countryman and Japan Cup rival Waverley Star in the Cox Plate—is being freely described as the best race many Australians have ever seen.

Big-time flat racing is reaching the stage where many believe only the megabuck can survive. Even the marvellous carnival jamboree of the Melbourne Cup on Tuesday resulted in a triumph for an expensive Arab-owned, Kentucky-bred colt. Everyone likes investment, and a Maktoum involvement would be a boon for Australian horsemen.

But racing needs its Davids as well as the Goliaths. Step forward, then, Bonecrusher: you are going to warm Dame Edna's heart.

Bonecrusher's Japanese challenge foundered with a nasty case of food poisoning which all but killed him. It made the main news bulletins back home because he had become a national hero. With 13 wins from more than 20 races he had earned it. Our flat-race stars in Britain have had much more fleeting fame over the last few years. The relationship with the public can go sour. It did a bit in 1989.

Nashwan: farewell to a fallen idol
October 22nd 1989

It is the love affair that died. Through the summer, the only arguments were how high Nashwan could be rated in the pantheon of champions. Now he is just another fallen Classic winner set for private duties in the breeding shed.

How could it be? Did not grown men weep when Willie Carson, in those bright blue silks, was led back to greet the wheelchair-bound "Major" after the Two Thousand Guineas in May?

Didn't Dick Hern say the big chestnut was the best of all the champions he had trained?

Wasn't Nashwan the first animal ever to complete the Two Thousand Guineas–Derby–Eclipse–King George four-timer in the same season?

Can one defeat on the treacherous turf at Longchamp finish what was hailed as the Horse of the Decade?

Well, it was always a dangerously fevered romance. In early April he was only a name on the Derby betting lists. By the end of it he was almost

Nashwan the Wonder Horse, and he had still to shake a leg in public this season.

The Dick Hern operation at West Ilsley is the last of the old, tight-lipped, it's-our-own-business school of training stables. But they could not keep this one quiet and Hern, beleaguered by the furore of the ending of his royal tenancy, found himself in the uncharacteristic position of being a "friend of the press".

One particular gallop in the middle of April is already into legend, and normal exaggeration should have Nashwan actually breaking the sound barrier before the story gets much older. So astonishing was his performance that the journey back from the Downs was one of acute discomfort for stable staff bursting to divest themselves of this knowledge to appreciative listeners, and it took only a couple of hours for Nashwan's Two Thousand Guineas price to shrink from 20-1 to 7-1.

The expectation was such that when Nashwan finally won the Guineas (albeit narrowly) it was like a coronation. By the time he ran away with the Derby a month later, we were already into jubilee-style celebrations, and things continued in this happily uncritical vein as Nashwan then slugged home in the Eclipse and followed up with a much closer call in the King George.

If we had wanted to look for it, the strain of this unique quartet of victories was already beginning to show. But we didn't care, this was "our" Nashwan. We had measured his giant, 33-foot stride, and Willie Carson had said that the sensation of full power was an almost sexual excitement. This was Superhorse, the new heavyweight champ. As far as we were concerned, he should appear every month and pummel some other luckless quadruped for our delight.

But then the idyll began to turn sour. Sheikh Hamdan, his owner, said that Nashwan would not be risked as a four-year-old. The St Leger was bypassed for a trial on the Arc de Triomphe track at Longchamp. Nashwan travelled badly, and with his long stride held by the soft ground met his first defeat. The Champion Stakes was billed as a finale, but cynics said we would never see the summer champion again, and on Tuesday night Dick Hern admitted that the horse was sick; after just seven races, Nashwan's public career was over.

Sadly, there is now a slight sense of resentment about Nashwan's achievements. There is a nasty feeling that everyone might have got a bit carried away earlier in the year, that Nashwan never beat very much and that his connections, by quitting when they are still ahead, have denied us next season's chance of discovering the truth. It is simpler and kinder to be realistic. By hustling his colt off to stud, his owner has denied Nashwan the chance of being compared with Nijinsky, Mill Reef or Brigadier Gerard, who spread their top-class form over at least two seasons. By invoking every

The stride of a champion. Willie Carson on Nashwan in full flow. Trainer, Dick Hern, called him poetry in motion (Trevor Jones)

superlative in the lexicon, we hacks built an unearned and unwanted aura around an immature three-year-old which was bound to end in tears.

But Willie Carson isn't crying, and he is not apologising, either. "If people want to knock him now, that's up to them," he said after racing on Thursday. "Nashwan beat the best around, you can't do more than that. But we 'bottomed' him in the Eclipse—he had to do something fantastic to catch Opening Verse—and after that I was having to look after him in the King George."

It was the end of the day, and there was rain in the wind. Mr Carson was changed into blazer and slacks, and the tic in his cheek was working as he thought back to the moments the world shared with Nashwan earlier in the year. "Look," he said defiantly. "I know what it felt like. He's still the best I've ever ridden."

Poor old Nashwan. By his sons we will have to judge him. That's not a criterion we can ever apply to Desert Orchid. We don't have to. The nation lost its heart to him long ago.

Rural rides: King Dessie on his annual progress
November 12th 1989

England our England, only weeks away from the space-age, Euro-conscious 1990s, and yet the outstanding sporting figure of the moment is a horse. Think on these things.

Maybe it is not so surprising. For although Desert Orchid seemed to have become, at nearly 11, a shade whiter at Wincanton on Thursday, his real attraction is that he is brilliant, brave and, in sporting terms, the ultimate green.

The Desert Orchid phenomenon, which has already spawned three books, two videos, a fan club and a phone line, is fuelled by a yearning for older, simpler, almost rustic values.

Desert Orchid cannot say he is sick as a parrot, or that he won't be quoted until you have talked to his agent. As a gelding, he is unlikely to make the nookie sections of the tabloid press. He just sets his great grey head off towards the fences and invites you to throw your spirit with him.

Thursday was what the racing papers call his seasonal debut. It was also a return to the heartland. Soft Somerset countryside, a crowd in weatherproof browns and greens knowing what they had come for, horse-lovers as much as punters every one.

So at first sight this was just a typical market-day Wincanton outing. Local people come to watch local horses, already a touch of cider in the voice. But then you saw the film crews and the journos and you realised that something was up. It might be a provincial stage, but there is no anonymity for a superstar.

In fact, we media hounds provided more than a touch of comic relief. There were film crews filming film crews filming film crews filming Desert Orchid. There were luckless hacks dispatched to ask earnest questions of long-bored connections. There were wonderfully unnecessary scuffles to get close to a target that you couldn't miss at midnight.

For Desert Orchid is a ham. He may not be able to read all those gushing superlatives in the cuttings book, but he knows that when he walks towards a crowd, wild-eyed people jump in front of him with clicking cameras, and the rest grin in silly wonderment and murmur to each other: "Doesn't he look great!"

Into the paddock he came, ears pricked, alert on parade, but with a look of satisfaction that the ratios of oohs and ahs was up to scratch for that stage of the season. With his immaculately plaited mane, his smart black rug, and little Janice Coyle marching neatly at his head, Desert Orchid almost looked the cardboard horse on a million cards this Christmas. But then he gave a half-buck and kicked out a hind leg like a boxer shadow-punching, and you realised he had come to fight.

Opposite: A star with his audience. Who says that horses don't have groupies too? (Chris Smith)

137

That moment captivated all over again. In an increasingly fraudulent world, Desert Orchid stands out for inescapably brave and honest endeavour.

He had only one opponent this time, but there were still three-and-a-quarter miles to be galloped, 21 fences to jump; quite enough risks for an exhibition round.

For the traveller there were flashing comparisons with another, much hotter, far more crowded, paddock in Miami just five days before. It is not poor little Zilzal's fault that he was snatched off to stud after that Breeders' Cup defeat, but for all his precocious speed, his six-victory summer was but an overpaid teenage scholarship compared with the hammering old slog Desert Orchid had been through to win 27 of his 55 races before this demolition of the Scottish National hero, Roll-A-Joint.

There should be tension before a horse race, particularly one over fences, but on Thursday there was a feeling of almost false security which won't be repeated in the big days ahead. Dessie was there to do his thing. God must be in his heaven and all the chicks will fly.

Sure enough, the old wonder played the game. His new jockey, Richard Dunwoody, soon had the tune. "I let him run along over the first three fences to get the gas out of him," he said in boyish, gap-toothed delight. "Once he had settled he was marvellous. It was a real thrill to sit on him."

And to watch. They could squeeze only 4,000 in at Wincanton. Over the season, the numbers will stretch into millions as Desert Orchid goes out to do business (and risk his neck) at Sandown, Cheltenham, maybe even Liverpool. He is a winner, a leader, a battler for success, and if you had a pound for every time you heard, "He's almost human," it would be holiday time in Acapulco.

Yet there can be too much stress on the animal kingdom. Just before the last race, the loudspeaker announced: "David Elsworth would like to say a few words." Anxious hacks seized notebooks, ready for changes to Dessie's plans. They were disappointed.

Dessie's trainer was not there to talk about the white horse. His Wiltshire voice was paying a simple, moving tribute to Joe Kelly, a much-loved member of the West Country circuit who died last month. "Without him," David said, "there's been something missing this afternoon."

People should be more important than horses. Desert Orchid's pre-eminence contrasts with the frantic quest for human heroes. You could forget it at Wincanton, but we need more than a white horse to keep the world afloat.

Something extraordinary had happened five days before "Dessie"'s Wincanton reappearance. At peak time on Saturday night, Channel 4 viewers had been wrapped up in an epic battle between two American super horses, Sunday Silence and Easy Goer, in the Breeders' Cup at Gulf Stream Park, Miami.

You would never have thought the interest would travel. But being involved in the telecast from Florida that night was one of the greatest of racing memories. You can understand why, a month later, a trip to cover the ludicrously over-hyped Duran "fight" in Las Vegas, needed little re-routing to also visit that Breeders' Cup hero and the old marvel who trained him.

Pray Silence for the best horse on earth
December 17th 1989

An old man and a young horse, and the future still to run for. As the last year of the 1980s bleeds away, Charlie Whittingham and Sunday Silence deserve the centre stage.

Out in California they have answered the criticism that big-time flat racing has become a business where you cash in your reputation and retire as soon as you can. For Whittingham and his Kentucky Derby hero have shown that this end of the game can still belong to the sports as much as to the business pages.

They have won the money right enough. Sunday Silence has accumulated more than £2.7m in 1989, three-and-a-half times the record-breaking total of Nashwan, last season's English Derby winner.

But they have also stayed on the pitch. While Nashwan, after just seven races, gathers his as yet untested libido at Sheikh Hamdan's magnificent Shadwell Stud in Norfolk, Sunday Silence remains under Whittingham's clear-blue eye in Barn 70 at Hollywood Park, with 12 races already run and a truer legend in the making.

Despite being founded by Bing Crosby and others in the 1930s, the Hollywood Park racecourse is a far cry from filmland. Set next to the Forum, the vast circular stadium where the Lakers have weaved their way to basketball fame, and right under the landing path of the jets lumbering into Los Angeles International, the course is part of one of the most urban places on this earth.

Yet when you get through the gates (outside which you are strongly advised to keep doors locked, wallets empty and maybe guns at the ready), the feeling in that first barn, alone on the right, is strictly country.

Chattering leather-legged riding girls sit on straw bales awaiting their horses. From the stalls comes a sing-song mix of Spanish and Southern

A pair of tough cookies. Breeders' Cup hero Sunday Silence and the legendary Charlie Whittingham at Hollywood Park in December 1990 (Chris Smith)

voices as grooms prepare stamping thoroughbreds for the next exercise set.

And in the little cubicle office by the entrance the old man sits on a wooden chair and chews over the days ahead.

At 76, Charlie Whittingham is now the most revered as well as the most successful of all the world's top trainers. His 1989 earnings of £7m (three times greater than Michael Stoute, the British number one) may not match the money machine of the remarkable Wayne Lukas but even that American training phenomenon lauds Whittingham as the master.

"They are two fine horses," Wayne said in Miami last month on the eve of Sunday Silence's Breeders' Cup showdown with arch-rival Easy Goer. "But no one, anywhere, can bring a horse up to a big race as perfectly tuned as Charlie does."

If you thought the man himself would give any elaborate, technical answers in keeping with the super-scientific 1990s, you would be in for a disappointment. Whittingham just keeps close to his horses, listens to his staff, and keeps his own counsel.

Charlie would be horrified at the comparison, but he is a perfect racing example of Albert Einstein's dictum: "Everything should be made as simple as possible, but never simpler."

Of course he would shrug wearily at such intellectualising of his role, just as he gently puts down queries as to why he is at work by five o'clock every morning. "Hell," he says, "it just stops me being an old drunk."

He still stands tall and erect like the marine he once was. He talks learnedly to the vet in what looks like a mobile chemist's shop, but the real secret clearly lies in that all-seeing eye and the wisdom of experience which stretches way back to Tijuana in the 1930s.

It was those qualities that first brought him together with Sunday Silence, now rated the best horse he has ever trained. Whole chapters have already been written as to just how unprepossessing and unwanted Sunday Silence looked as a yearling. Whittingham will have none of it.

"Sure, he looked a bit weak and sickle-hocked," he said, looking at the lean black champion walking round the shed. "But I don't mind that. I liked the way he moved. He was like a cat. And when I first saw him gallop —I'll never forget it."

The words come gently. There is no need to impress. But Whittingham is adamant that it is Sunday Silence's free, floating action that has been the key to his three successes in those four epic duels with America's other champion, Easy Goer, duels which have lit up a nation far less interested in thoroughbred racing than our own.

"People out East want to blame the jockey or the tactics," Whittingham says of the New York-based Easy Goer. "And it's true he whipped us in the Belmont over a mile and a half. But we can make a move any time in a race, and over a mile and a quarter we are going to be too quick for him."

The next, much-awaited clash between two wonderful horses, neither of which has ever run worse than second, may not take place until next autumn's Breeders' Cup. Easy Goer has 12 wins from 17 runs; Sunday Silence 8 from 12 with the 13th unlikely to come earlier than May as he is at present on two months' walking recuperation after two little chips were removed from his right knee.

The horse walks soundly enough, and the only mark is some shaven hair at the points where the arthroscope was inserted. But you can see the ribs along his quite narrow flank. "Yes, we want him light," Charlie said quietly. "That's why we kept him here, and didn't send him away to the farm.

"The last thing you want is for him to get heavy and studdish," he added. "We'll build him up, but we'll build him with muscle. And we'll take anyone on."

An old warrior with a great horse, not frightened to pitch him on to the racetrack. With stud values in this country so much higher than rewards on the racecourse, Whittingham's approach with Sunday Silence does not often prevail here.

Our attitude may be understandable, even wise, but it still amounts to a fear of losing. And the fear of losing betrays the very essence of sport whether you are in it for a billion dollars or just the beer.

Out West there's an old man and a tall black horse who can still dream our dream.

There was an unhappy postscript to Sunday Silence's story. Charlie Whittingham got him back into racing shape. He worked brilliantly, won again on the track. But first his old rival Easy Goer broke down, then his own legs also gave way. The pair had done us proud but their owners' perseverance cost them one year's earning on the stallion roster. Forty mares at $100,000 a time, it was quite a sacrifice.

Finally, a story which takes us back to the jumping game, to Ireland and to the shrine for the horse they still call "Himself". There will only ever be one Arkle. But when that same tranquil stable in County Dublin housed an animal who on his day could give the rest of the nation's nags a start and a beating, you couldn't blame the whole country for shutting its eyes in hope.

The heavy burden of Irish dreams
February 25th 1990

It may need a miracle. Ireland still dreams of Cheltenham Gold for Carvill's Hill, but first we'll have to find some magic to fix his back.

On Thursday it was "a whole lot better" according to Nicky O'Connor, Carvill's devoted Lad these past four seasons. But this did not stop the big horse looking uncomfortable as the O'Connor fingers ran down his spine.

Therein lies another problem. If Carvill's Hill was in real form, he would not so much look uncomfortable as ears-back ferocious.

"He's being almost reasonable at the moment," said Patricia Dreaper, his trainer's wife as their horse threatened O'Connor with a well-practised set of teeth. "That means he's lost some spark. When he's right he really hates people."

The weight of history. Did we all expect too much of Carvill's Hill? (Chris Smith)

If he knew what they were saying he would hate them even more. For Carvill's Hill has got himself saddled with a burden heavier than any handicap ever set.

He carries with him the expectation of the Irish, a yearning to put the clock back to other times when the shamrock reigned supreme. It is a load that would cripple even an elephant.

What's worse, Carvill's Hill is so tantalisingly close to the real thing. He even lives in the right place. As he posed for our photographs on Thursday, he was standing where Arkle stood.

It's now a quarter of a century since the days of the greatest steeplechaser anyone has ever seen but the Dreaper yard has hardly changed a jot.

True, there is rather more traffic on the winding Ashbourne to Swords road, and the jets are a whole lot bigger at Dublin Airport, 10 miles away to the south.

But the feel is the same, unspoilt in a spoiling world.

There never was anything fancy about those red doors, the whitewashed stables, and the big hay-barn at the back where we loosed the horses for a roll after exercise.

No one used to get very excited, the tone set by old Tom Dreaper himself, a soft, ageless unimpressed wisdom about him, usually referring to horses by their box numbers; Arkle was "No. 7" and Flyingbolt "that big chestnut". His son Jim tasted the big time early: at 20 he was second in the Grand National at Liverpool.

After his father's death he trained Ten Up to land the Gold Cup, and Brown Lad to win twice at Cheltenham. Since then the luck has ebbed and flowed, some of the old wells have run dry, but perspective has never been lost. Not even with Carvill's Hill.

You can't blame the dreamers, particularly not when you are in the export trade.

Some big raking five-year-old has only to win a couple of races with his mouth open for the dog-eared "best since Arkle" label to be stuck on his bridle complete with a six-figure price tag for an English owner. Carvill's Hill is the one that did not go away.

Although he did change hands between John Lilley and Maeve McMorrow in his early days, he has remained at Kilsallaghan, his present owner refusing offers that would have settled the national debt on the simple premise that "money can't buy a horse who might win the Gold Cup".

At last the country has a contender to call her own.

But this is a flawed Irish genius in the great tradition. There was never any doubting the potential of the tall 17-hand recruit even if Jim Dreaper did at first call him "one of the ugliest horses I have ever seen".

Two wins in amateur riders "bumper" flat races alerted the scouts, four hurdle successes got the headlines ready and when he finally went over fences last season the dreams were almost overcooked.

For it was soon clear that you could take this horse to fences but you could not always make him jump.

In just 15 months he has already won seven steeplechases but moments of breathtaking power have been mixed with sudden lapses of gruesome ineptitude.

He fell in last year's Gold Cup when second favourite to Desert Orchid and still had his supporters head-shaking at his errors when he finally got on the course this season.

The reasons are well chronicled but no easier for that. Carvill's Hill is such a long-striding "Too-Tall Jones" of a horse that adjusting his stride for a fence is always going to be a problem. Add a delicate back and a cantankerous temperament that threatened water-borne destruction during one soon abandoned attempt at swimming therapy, and you have problems enough to send any trainer grey.

Jim Dreaper has not got many silver threads but Nicky O'Connor is coming to the end of 33 years with the stable; he even led out Arkle one day at Fairyhouse.

Nicky knows the game but is not abandoning hope just yet. "The public have never seen what this horse can really do," he said, adjusting Carvill's rug with cautious respect.

"He may not be Arkle or Flyingbolt, but I rate him up with Brown Lad and Leap Frog, them sort of hosses. He was a bit disappointing last Saturday but at least his jumping was much better."

Which leads us to the "busted flush" theory now freely available from Carvill's Hill's detractors. "What's the excuse this time?" asked one such from the safe haven of the committee bar at windswept Downpatrick on Wednesday.

"Last Saturday at Leopardstown the horse jumped perfectly but got well beaten by Nick The Brief, the first half-decent English horse he has ever met. He's all hype."

Jim Dreaper was also north of the border on Wednesday, at Downpatrick to saddle something in the first.

He has been around much too long to get involved in arguments about his champion. "In reality it's pretty hopeless. The back will always be a problem and last week the horse wasn't really firing properly either.

"In a perfect world we would stop and start all over again next season. But we know how good he can be, we have got three weeks, so we might as well have a go."

The sun was still out, a good crowd was beginning to file in, a tribute to the vitality which has kept the little course alive against all the odds.

Jim Dreaper looked across at the track's eccentric, big-dipper contours, thought of all the pre-Cheltenham talk up ahead, and maybe also of rather larger problems that this beautiful troubled land has had to survive.

He summed it up sweetly. "What the hell," he said. "It's only a horse race."

Carvill's Hill didn't make it to Cheltenham and for all his talent looks destined to be remembered as a "might have been". But like all the others he had something. Something to lift the spirit, prick the wallet. Something to hitch that wagon to.

Not an expert but an enthusiast. Down the years I have always been drawn to the theatre of sport across all its disciplines. To the commitment and pressure and fulfilment that the stars draw from their forte. Here are some views along the way.

The first comes from the often refined-looking world of show-jumping. Refined, that is, for those who observe it from the politer side of the TV screen. Up close it is a much harsher game, and none the worse for it. Go north and see.

The roughrider of Craiglands Farm
February 3rd 1985

The face is like the landscape: craggy, windswept, unsubdued. The man is like his horses; he doesn't walk through life, he kicks it on the rump. High up on the Yorkshire moors above Bingley, Harvey Smith, the old V-sign himself, is ready for another season.

This month the unpronounceable Dutch town of s'Hertogenbosch will see showjumping's first World Cup event of 1985, and with it the beginning of Harvey Smith's 28th year in international competition. Once again the great arenas of the world will be illuminated by the jutting jaw, the massive hands and the beetlebrowed competitiveness of the most professional Yorkshireman of them all. But if you want to understand why Harvey has become a landmark, not just in his own sport but across the face of British life, you must get up Ilkley way and back to basics.

Great jagged rocks stick up through the fields on the way to the moor, and Craiglands Farm makes about as many concessions to aesthetics as its owner does to gentlemen's tailoring. Leeds and its big-city planning may be only 10 miles away through the valleys, but up here, when you get out of the wind and into the kitchen to find a lumberjack-shirted Harvey talking to his two huge and massively talented sons, it feels so like some pioneer's cabin on the edge of the Rockies that you half expect to see a grizzly at the window.

On through into the living-room, and you see some of the trophies that mark the straightforward public side of the 47-year-old bricklayer's son from nearby Eldwick whose arrival into the well-bred world of showjumping was one of the great comic dramas of our time. There are the four Hickstead Derbys, the seven John Player Trophies and enough horse statuettes to put a knick-knack shop out of business.

But there's also a green parrot called Reggie who sings God Save the Queen to remind us of the zanier side of things: that Harvey Smith is the only leading sportsman who's also been a professional wrestler and a stand-up comedian—25 nights last February from Inverness to Hastings—from stag nights to (heaven help them!) Ladies' Literary evenings.

The most famous joke of all is commemorated by a brass knocker on the kitchen door in the shape of two fingers pointing skywards in that same V-sign that was raised in "up yours" triumph at the directors' box when he heard he had won the Hickstead Derby in 1971. Today, 800 acres spread across the hill mean that there is no longer any need for chips on those great knotted shoulders, but when he takes you outside to see the horses you are back into the pioneering times again.

For inside the two huge, gloomy, grey barns, there is no gleaming array of boxes with horses standing like polished guardsmen at the ready. No, most of Harvey's 37 nags are corralled Western style in two great pens where they eat, play, fight and sleep just as if they were on the ranch a century ago.

"People think I am mad having them all in together," said Harvey, catching some enormous thing by the tail to cue it into a circus lie-down trick. "But they are herd animals, and like this they are much happier, much more pleased to see you. What's more," he added with a sly wink, "they are much fitter. You'll see."

So it was that half an hour later I was hoisted aboard some great bay brute, and bidden to follow Ilkley's answer to Beau Brummel across his beloved moors for what he described as "a nice blow". Seeing that my horse had enough reins and straps around its head to winch a tank into a troopship, and hearing Harvey's proud boast that the beast "hadn't been out of those pens for seven weeks", it looked like we were into the trickiest test of manhood since a rabbit-shooting jaunt with "Big Jack" Charlton and the dread words, "It's your turn now, kid."

Despite one frightful moment when it seemed as if the next stop would be the mill chimneys of Bradford in the distance, we survived the gallop to walk back alongside the master and hear a lecture on future plans and present economics. "I've always been commercially minded," said Harvey. "That's what's good about Sanyo, my present sponsors. They pay me a fee for my services. The horses carry their name in the ring, but they are still mine to sell, and every horse has its price."

It then transpired that I had the honour of riding Sanyo Technology who, with two other "good 'uns", will carry Harvey at the aforementioned s'Hertogenbosch in two weeks' time. Three other Sanyo "specials" will have 23-year-old Robert Smith aboard to start a season in which Harvey says he will consider himself a match "for any booger in't world". But before then, other family work was calling, and back in the barns four bemused-looking Middle Eastern gentlemen were sitting on a bench watching Robert and his younger brother Stephen (silver medal at Los Angeles) jump some horses with a view to sale.

At first it seemed a simple opportunity for Harvey's sense of showmanship ("I love theatre, we should get more of it into show jumping"), but then, when he himself climbed aboard with that famous "Desperate Dan" look, a remark by Stephen Smith suggested that Harvey had something else besides energy and ego to keep him on course. "Oh, he's all right, our Dad," said Stephen with a grudging smile, "but Robert's the best now. He's got such style he's poetry in motion. Dad's still great when he's an underdog, but he's an old man now and his style is like mine, a bit rough and ready."

On Harvey's range, they definitely don't eat quiche.

At the very least Harvey has had a tremendously long life in his own field. In other sports the expectation is much shorter—and a lot more brutal.

In June 1986, along with a gaggle of expectant British Press, I made the pilgrimage to Caesar's Palace, Las Vegas, in the hope of witnessing another winning chapter in what had up to then been the glorious, heart-warming saga of Barry McGuigan, the little charmer from Northern Ireland who won a world title but spoke of wider things. He even had a dove on his flag and called himself a "warrior for peace".

In still early evening (to ensure live British TV coverage) and therefore in sauna-bath heat, McGuigan took a beating which brought a sadness far beyond any normal boxing defeat. There was the sense that something quite exceptional was over. It seemed to reach right back to the little border town where it had all begun.

Barry: requiem for a featherweight
June 29th 1986

The rain was falling on Clones, but the mood was one of bitterness, not tears. A bedraggled blue flag across the street read: Barry, King of the Ring. No Nevada nightmare would change it yet.

Outside the general store, a stuffed parrot quipped: "Have you got your credit card?" Inside, Barry McGuigan's mother, Katie, was slicing bacon. She's a bright, spare, bespectacled little woman of 50 whose head comes up motherhen-wise in defence of any of her eight-strong brood. "They are all special to me," she said. "But obviously at this time it's Barry who concerns us. And what happened out there I cannot forgive."

Fifty yards away at the Lennard Arms (subtitled the Barry McGuigan Supporters Club), Barry's mother-in-law, Joan Mealiff, took time off from her family hotel-keeping duties to echo the general feeling of resentment. "We all think Las Vegas must be a cod of a place," she said. "Barry should never have been taken to fight in that heat. If he could come back here to fight one more time, he would show the world what he's made of."

The nicest thing about the village of Clones is that, despite being right on the troubled Northern Ireland border, it gives off a feeling of clan-caring friendliness. Little wonder that they should be upset when their most famous son took such a frying on Monday night. Little surprise that they blame everything except their own heart-stirring hero.

But that's not how it seemed in Nevada. Granted all that has been chronicled about the 110-degree heat, the supposed problems at the weigh-in, the three-point deduction for a low blow, the sun in the eyes; to this, admittedly inexperienced, ringside observer, there was no denying that something was lacking.

Don't say it's hindsight, because my tattered notebook has the sweat on it still. It records that even before the first eyeball-to-eyeball "when I say break, I mean break" referee confrontation, it had been Cruz's composure rather than McGuigan's scowling concentration that caught the eye. The 22-year-old challenger skipped easily, head high, his perfectly muscled torso gleaming a dark chestnut in the sun. The 25-year-old champion shadow-boxed intently, taller, craggier, but with a hint of rib beneath the pinched white skin, a touch of the war-torn warrior about the face.

Despite a determined McGuigan opening, the second round (given to Cruz on all three judges' scorecards) did little to dispel those early premonitions. Then, although the much-awaited Clones (it's pronounced Clo-ness) Cyclone blew up to the extent that the notebook says, "McGuigan in control," a left hook from Cruz in the sixth brought such wobble-legged signs of fallibility that an old hand dictating round-by-round to London cupped the telephone and shouted, "We're in the shit!"

McGuigan going backwards was a terrible sight, like an animal moving against its nature. But for those sixth and seventh rounds (both lost on all cards), backwards he went, desperate to avoid damage far more serious than that inflicted by the heat. From then on it was clearly uphill for Barry. There were eight rounds ahead, and it's a measure of his achievement that all three judges gave him at least five.

But he lost the fight; because of a simple, three-knock-down truth. In the 10th, and twice in that terrible final 15th, the number nine contender landed punches on the McGuigan chin which some claim were heat-assisted or championship-inspired, but which either way reduced Barry to a

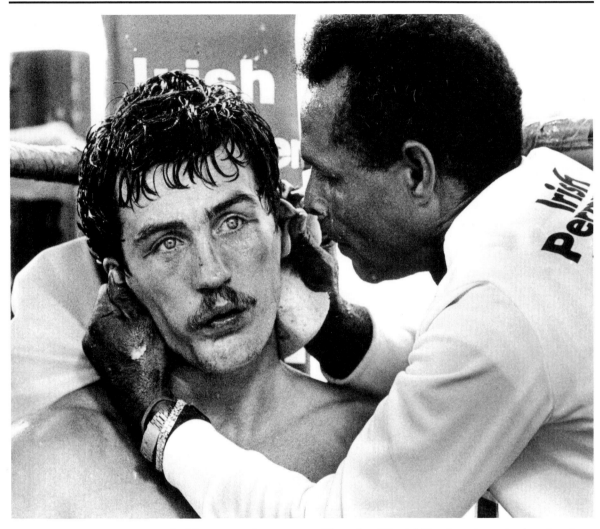

Beyond repair. Barry McGuigan in his darkest hour. Las Vegas, 1986 (Chris Smith)

crumpled heap on the canvas. That the World Boxing Association featherweight champion got up and stayed afloat will remain the most defiant triumph of mind over matter that this observer has ever seen. But it still confirmed that while the spirit remained super-willing, the flesh had become weak.

That view didn't receive much shrift from the Clones team in the Lennard Arms on Thursday night, nor indeed from some distinguished boxing brains who affirm that the conditions were all. Time to bring in the bad goblin in these arguments, McGuigan's long-time manager, Barney Eastwood, who had opened the Caesars Palace poolside press conference on Tuesday with the unlikely assertion that "the heat was not a factor", and who was in equally unrepentant mood back home near Belfast on Friday.

"All I can be accused of," said Eastwood, "is of taking up a little boy from the country and helping his extraordinary determination, but not great boxing ability, towards a world championship and, I might say, to a financial situation where he can be comfortably off for the rest of his days."

Eastwood volunteered more: "Barry always wanted to get the very best money. To do that he had to go to America. Of course he would have beaten Cruz over here, but he wouldn't have looked impressive, and he would have earned a quarter of the cash [over $1m gross last week]. In my opinion, he has gone downhill since he won the championship. He trains too hard, and at the very least should take a long, long rest."

We're into technical areas now, so let's return to a vivid Las Vegas memory. At the end of things, McGuigan put his arm around his enemy and was carried off a mental and physical wreck. Next fight on was the latest, maybe closing, chapter in the once-great career of Roberto Duran. He took a beating, but it was a split decision. At the closing bell there was no embrace, just a dismissive, wild-dog snarl.

You can only paint pictures as you see them. For me, Barry McGuigan has worked in the devil's kitchen for some time. He has done much for others to savour, won big money for himself and his family. There's no shame, and much merit, in leaving it now.

McGuigan didn't take the outsider's advice but he was never the same again. It was 18 months before he was in the ring, a four-fight come-back at a heavier weight which went off the rails against the unsung Jim McDonnell. Barry wisely moved on with his charm and most of his fortune intact.

At his height he had something very special, a national head of steam that made you feel that anything was possible. Of course any great player at their peak is a thrill to watch. Even if you are 8,000 miles from home and have never seen them or their game before.

No quarter given by the gladiators
November 29th 1987

The search is for the absolute. Sometimes sport can give it in blurred moments of brilliance which sear in the memory. It was like that when John Elway played at Los Angeles Coliseum on Sunday.

Down on the pitch the noise took you straight back to the days of ancient Rome. The speed and impact of massive player on massive player would have made a gladiator gulp. But Elway, the Denver Broncos quarterback, was the sporting ultimate. You couldn't take your eyes off him.

American Football buffs will know that John Elway, 26, 6ft 3in and 15st, is now rated the best in the business, and has just received a five-year, $12m contract. But this is written by a first-time observer of the old colony's national game, and after Sunday's Los Angeles Raiders-versus-Broncos baptism of fire, I am still in aftershock. The whole thing was terrifying, but Elway transformed it.

The real superstars impress you even at the walk. Mill Reef was the best I have ever seen, but he was a four-legged phenomenon. On two, there was Bobby Moore, with that wonderful confidence-giving bow-legged step; Greg Norman has a magnificent strutting march, and I once followed his fellow Australian, Evonne Goolagong, the length of Los Angeles Airport to observe her perfect, padding, heel-and-toe balance. But none of them compares with Elway.

Fifty other players were on the pitch. The cheerleaders, the Raiderettes, were waving and flouncing away for the black-shirted home team. Different groups of heavily padded, white-breeched Broncos huddled into hand-in-the-centre psyched-up groups, and around them, shoulder shifting, neck turning, stalked the quarterback.

Under the helmet there was a fair, blue-eyed, quite open face. But it's a slow, rolling, infinitely self-confident walk, and let me tell you that if he kicked the saloon-bar door open, everyone would dive for cover.

Despite the sunshine, there were clouds in the air. The Raiders had lost six games in a row, a situation a lot more serious than the 6.3 earthquake which made my hotel room jump on Tuesday. Every one of the 60,000 crowd wanted to bust the Broncos and, as Denver rely to an extreme extent on Elway, that meant to "sack" the quarterback.

Other sports give huge responsibilities. A motor-racing driver is in more danger, has to use more specific, test-pilot-like skills; a soccer midfield star has a more constant 90-minute involvement; but for the quarterback there is a double pressure. Only he can make things happen, and every time he has to combat some of the world's largest, quickest and most dangerous men intent on homicide.

The pressure never hung heavy on Elway. Only once in three hours did the opposing "dee-fense" get to him as, arm-cocked, he loped backwards and sideways away from the line of scrimmage looking for a teammate free. Then "whoomph", the arm came across and the ball went to its target as if it had heat-seeking guidance. "He could," says Dick Enberg, the most warmly intelligent of all American sportscasters, "throw a strawberry through a locomotive."

Naturally, a Raiders–Broncos game involves a lot more than one man, and the emotions ran through the cheerful early optimism of the peanut

The golden arm. At his peak, John Elway could throw a pass like a laser beam (Chris Smith)

seller who could chuck a packet inch-perfect five rows deep, to the stricken face of the Raiders coach Tom Flores at the final score, so dark in thought and fury that not one player, let alone a paparazzo, dared go near him as he walked to the tunnel.

And there was a sublime moment that Raiders fans will replay till next winter. Their one ace is a black shell called Bo Jackson who has been timed through 40 yards in 4.19 seconds, which means that if you wound the Coliseum clock back 55 years to its 1932 Olympics, you could have backed Jackson off the board to win the 100 metres in full football gear.

Bo likes to call himself a part-timer—all summer he plays top baseball for Kansas City. But there wasn't anything amateur about the way he came around the left side in the third quarter of the game. Between him and the line was the 6ft 1in, 13½st Mike Harden, acclaimed as Denver's best defensive player. Bo is also 6ft 1in. He weighs 16½st, and he didn't mess about. At full tilt he bulled straight into Harden's shoulder, knocked him flat and dived over for a touchdown.

It's a hard, hard game, and one of the injuries was unhappily prophetic. "Steve Sewell is such a big target," said the Broncos coach, Dan Reeves, the night before, "that I wonder about keeping him healthy." Sewell, the wide receiver, may be 6ft 3in and 15½st, but they broke his jaw despite the helmet.

So the man who rules has special gifts. Down there on the pitch, when the ball whips back to Elway from the scrimmage, there is suddenly an intense, flashing, almost addictive violence as his guards try to defend him from the hell-fire of his opponents. There's no slow-roll in the stride now, but the power of the cocked arm is still deadly in its confidence. Just as you think a dreadful "sack" is imminent, the arm draws back and the ball goes a full 35 yards, laser flat, bullet fast, smack into the hands of a sprinting receiver. Yes, it was the ultimate.

Elway's hot streak continued through Superbowl '88 until his dreadful Armageddon against Joe Montana and the 49ers in the Superbowl rout of 1990.

The power of television took that game all round the world; American football has become much more than just an American interest. So too the Tour de France, now screened all over Europe and beyond. Like American football, it was much more exciting in the flesh. I will go a lot further than that. This first exposure to the "Tour" was the best single sporting experience I have ever had as a spectator. What a day!

Mountain men with wings on their wheels
July 23rd 1989

Nothing can prepare you for the big day in the mountains. To watch the riders on the Tour de France up close just takes your breath away. They must have wings on their wheels.

The enormity of what happened across three peaks and 100 sweat-soaked miles in the Hautes Alpes on Wednesday was quite incredible enough. But that the 150 *coureurs* who set off from Briançon's old ramparts that morning should have already put in more than 70 hours and 1,825 miles during 16 days in the saddle, challenges all ordinary notions about the limits of human endurance.

Only the day before they had ended a 108-mile stage by climbing out above the tree line in 40-degree heat for the final ascent of the 7,742ft Col d'Isoard before plunging at breakneck speed down another 3,000 feet in a descent that would keep sensible motorists in low gear.

The fact that the Tour began back in 1903, and that the legends of the past have all tackled these seemingly insuperable tasks only added to the expectation as the sun began to cook the cool mountain air on Wednesday. Indeed, most of the old heroes were here; Merckx, Hinault, Poulidor, and Bahamontes, the great Spaniard whose climbing exploits in the early sixties won him that most evocative of nicknames, the Eagle of Toledo.

(Photo: Chris Smith)

The experts agreed that Wednesday's would be the stage to decide the tour, whose 21st and final stage ends in the Champs-Elysées this afternoon. The American Greg Lemond, hero of 1986, held the overall leader's yellow jersey, but only by 53sec from Laurent Fignon, the French 1983 and 1984 winner, with the Spaniard Pedro Delgado a further 1min 55sec away and desperate to get back to the ruthless mountain form that won him the Tour last year.

Insiders had it that Fignon who, with his rimless glasses and long blond pigtail, looks more like a mad scientist than a super athlete, was struggling to hold his place and that it was the blue-eyed, almost baby-faced, Delgado who could break the clean-cut Lemond on the anvil of the closing 3,000ft climb to the ski resort of L'Alpe d'Huez.

It was 10.15 and the place was abuzz by the time the big three had walked to the registration book on the makeshift stage at Briançon. Like the others they seem strangely birdlike and out of their element on foot, and in the strange hovering way they slow-ride their bikes around the paddock area, shaking the odd hand, signing an autograph, loading water bottles on to the cycle frame, stuffing bananas and nectarines into their pockets. These are men bearing the scars of two weeks on the road, but from their honed cheek-bones to their shaved, elegantly muscled legs, these are creatures who also have to fly to survive.

Until *in extremis*, they move in flocks. At first, long, wheeling arrows of men and machines spin the length of the Guisane valley to the bottom of the massive Col de Galibier. Then a 20-strong group detaches itself as the endlessly ascending hairpins begin to bite, and closer to the top of this 10-mile, 3,000ft climb the wild-eyed Dutchman Gert Theunisse breaks clear with two others to lead over the 8,661ft peak.

Just pedalling up Galibier is achievement enough for the many splendid amateur cyclists who are part of the 50,000 crowd draped around the mountain. But the men of the tour are professionals. They are just a fifth of the way through this day's journey. And it shows.

Once over the summit, they are businesslike, not breathless. With almost synchronised movements they zip up their jerseys with the right hand, change down the gears with the left and then sweep the same hand behind their backs for the water bottle to prime themselves for the descent.

Now the visitor again dives deep into disbelief. These would be black runs on a ski map. The riders wing down them at over 60mph, and there is 6,000 feet to lose.

Round the precipice-sided hairpins they go, on through little wooden villages *en fête*, down forest glens, over dizzy gorges, out eventually into the valley and then incongruously on to the wide main road that connects the village of Saint-Michel to the cathedral town of Saint-Jean de Maurienne further down the River Arc.

A suicidal Italian called Franco Vona got clear of the field down the worst of the descent, but he has been gobbled up by Saint-Jean, and as they begin to work against the collar the bunch around Lemond's yellow jersey still includes Delgado and Fignon. Soon the Spaniard has to make it hurt.

To get this far, our accredited press car has had to endure the risky delights of the longest one-way road in the world, the closed route of the Tour de France. We toboggan down perilous slopes while being overtaken by hell-bent journalists from foreign lands. We battle up people-strewn paths, and finally park for a sandwich three-quarters of the way up the Croix de Fer.

It is two o'clock, some three hours into the stage, and tar-meltingly hot. But any thought of respite for mere spectators is scotched when the binoculars reveal some tiny figures toiling up the empty road behind the flashing lights of the police outriders. The wonderment of their being so close behind our still throbbing car calls for an exact double take of the line in the Butch Cassidy film, when Paul Newman looks down the valley at his pursuers and says bitterly: "Who are those guys?"

The questions are getting very brutal. Theunisse, his long hair hanging over the collar of his polka-dotted King of the Mountains jersey, launches himself clear of the pack into the teeth of the climb. Behind him the dozen riders around Lemond have to reach deep into the locker, but it is only the little Frenchman, Charly Mottet, who looks like losing his grip.

The summit of Croix de Fer is 6,779ft. Ahead lie 25 miles whirling down through the valley of the Romansche before the last great pull, 21 hairpins up to 6,100ft at L'Alpe d'Huez. Somehow everyone knew it had to come to this.

Ten kilometres to go and the big three are still locked together four minutes off Theunisse. This is straight suffering now. There are only five of them in the group. Delgado's Colombian teammate, Rondon, sets the pace and the stars will have to reach into their very souls to attack.

Delgado owes himself this after last year's doping scandal and the inexplicable amnesia that made him late for the start three weeks ago. Lemond has come so far since the shooting accident that nearly crippled him in 1987 that if he can hold on now he should wear the yellow jersey all the way to Paris. Fignon has had two bad days; the pundits expect him to weaken. But he still feels strong and he has been here before.

They are almost five hours into the race. Half of France and most of Holland are hanging on to the hillside. Theunisse can win the stage, but only one of the big three can win the Tour. On Rondon grinds, 6km to the finish, 5km and then, at precisely 4km, the absolute moment of death.

Fignon looks across at Lemond and sees weakness in the American's pain-racked shoulders. With one titanic move of mind, muscle and self-

Wheel to wheel. Laurent Fignon (right) and Greg Lemond (opposite) worked to an astonishing show-down in the 1989 Tour de France (Chris Smith)

belief the Frenchman kicks out and away from the bunch. Delgado struggles after him, but Lemond has to let them go. Lemond, the yellow jersey, has cracked.

The crowd are going bananas. They know that if Fignon digs deep enough he can take the race lead for France. There is stupendous noise and people. Policemen try hopelessly to clear a way for the outriders and suddenly the cheers hit a high as a first figure comes through.

It is Theunisse, his eyes bulging, ferocious for the finish. The Dutchmen

bellow in triumph but the crowd know that the crucial test is who will appear next. It is two riders, a yellow-striped one in front. But it is not Lemond, it is Fignon. He has Delgado at his wheel, he has his mouth open in the agony of effort, but he will not weaken. He will win the Tour.

Soon afterwards he stands patiently through the victory ceremony before donning the yellow jersey. Laurent Fignon may look like a mad professor but on Wednesday evening his smile might almost have found the secret of life itself.

Well, Fignon had his moment, but four days later
Lemond took the Tour from him with that incredible
final time trial up the Champs Elysées, a blend of
muscle and machine driving itself beyond all
ordinary limits of man. It was 24.5km from Versailles
to Paris, Fignon had 51 seconds in hand. They were
not enough.

Of course both Lemond and Fignon were driven
men with no heed of later days when the body can no
longer take you out beyond. But those days will surely
come. They come to us all. They even came to Jonah
Barrington.

The tortured quest that left a mark on Jonah Barrington
October 29th 1989

What happens when the spirit is still willing but the flesh is getting weak? For Jonah Barrington, 49 next April, easing up doesn't seem to be an option.

That is good news for the game of squash into which he still pours more direct energy than any other British sportsman has generated in the last 20 years. But seeing him on Thursday you had to wonder how good it was for Jonah.

For at first glance Barrington looks something of a wreck. The player whose very name became synonymous with the sort of fanatical application which lifted him to World No. 1 in the 1960s and 1970s, the man who as director of excellence is the off-court force behind the British squash teams of the moment, no longer moves like the snarling leopard of another time.

At least not when his guard is down. Out on the road, he is still buzzing through clinics and exhibition matches for the Squash Rackets Association, for Dunlop and a host of other sponsors for the boys at Millfield School, to which he is attached. But sitting with his family in their ranch-style home at the foot of historic Glastonbury Tor you see the toll his battles have taken.

All sports demand their pound of flesh, some more brutally and immediately than others. Boxing had another hideous reminder of its risks when Rod Douglas ended on a life support machine this Thursday. The current rugby and National Hunt seasons are already keeping the casualty wards busy. But you don't associate battered bodies with squash. Well, not until you see Barrington.

It's not so much the hobbling walk which betrays the knee that finally gave way this summer, nor even the gaunt, rather stooping figure which recalls all those titanic struggles in the torture chamber into which Jonah converted squash courts for both himself and his opponents. It's the face that tells the tale.

For in repose there is a weariness, a sadness almost, about the hawk-thin features. The famous Viva Zapata moustache of the unstoppable ego-filled era is shaven to reveal a straight ascetic upper lip. The heavy-lidded brown eyes still blaze with interest but there are shadows beneath them.

There is desperate irony here. For at his wonderful storm-cracking peak Jonah represented the very breath of life. His was the intrusive, classless figure who proclaimed that with will and application anything was possible. To meet him then was to feel the force and think it would never stop. Now you feel it all right but wonder how long it can continue.

This is to fill the page with the "negative thoughts" which Jonah has always branded as the enemy. But it is also to face up to a dilemma which spreads beyond Barrington to life itself. If the waves that have been your energy begin to erode the cliffs that have been your strength, how do you re-structure the act in middle age?

Over the last month it was his version of "accentuate the positive, eliminate the negative" that Barrington thundered into the British players' ears in the sweat-filled 90-second mid-match intervals in the world championships in Singapore and Kuala Lumpur. You wouldn't have thought that this

The story is in the face. Jonah Barrington has brought a unique commitment to his sport but the body is taking the toll (Chris Smith)

demanded a training schedule that would knacker an Olympian in his prime. But that is the standard Jonah has set himself and like the whale that swallowed his namesake, he cannot let it go.

"If I don't go through two training sessions a day, I cannot measure up to what the public are entitled to expect," he said. "They and my sponsors still want to see me in shape. I have got to do this to keep myself together. I worry what would happen if I couldn't perform."

It's not a wholly convincing explanation. Especially when you hear his wife, Madelaine, herself an Olympic athlete, talk about "the disease", and when one watcher in a gymnasium in Somerset reported seeing Barrington drive himself to quite inhuman limits on Wednesday afternoon.

What is doubly ironic is that Barrington himself recognises the dangers of excess, particularly amongst the teenagers to whom he has already been such an inspiration. He rails against the treadmill routines which have brought about the Tracy Austin early burn-out syndrome. Flashes of wit lighten the earnestness. "My sons have the best routine of all," he says over lunch. "They play the games in their seasons. They are wonderfully talented and all they say is, 'I don't want to be obsessive like Dad.'"

But for all the hammering that he takes on this personal anvil, there is no denying that Barrington as he comes to 50 remains a phenomenon which we and he really ought to harness. The Squash Rackets Association have moved the arch anti-bureaucrat from a two-month to a 21-month contract and Jonah is now touchingly anxious to get a five-year agreement. His aim is to finish the job started in 1979, to equip British squash players with something of the professionalism which he considers essential to compete at the highest level.

"It's a question of attitude, of establishing good habits," he says, warming to a favourite theme. "There are an awful lot of diversions for young people and they have to be prepared to do the work. You really can go a fantastic distance with willpower. When people talk about talent they so often don't register the talent inside the brain, that indefinable determination."

When he talks like this the whole room begins to crackle. "I am totally fascinated by the psychology of sport," he says. "Everyone can improve both their performance and enjoyment with effort, but real champions have to be prepared to suffer and their coaches have to be ready to set them an example.

"Before Herb Elliott won the gold medal in the Rome Olympics he was taken out to watch his coach Percy Cerutty nearly bust himself running a mile in almost five minutes. Cerutty was in his fifties but wanted to show him how much he cared. I think I can give a bit of that."

Afterwards he stood outside in the drizzle with the Tor behind him. A loner who has built a mystique about himself, in front of a ridiculously steep physical folly which has attracted good and bad myths down the ages.

The last abbot was hung from the roof of the hill-top monastery exactly 450 years ago. The old stories had it that the whole Tor was originally created to cover a trap door to Hades.

Some might think that Jonah himself is headed for the river of darkness. But remember that Glastonbury and the Tor were also said to have had King Arthur upon them. Barrington may be paying the price, but the energy still burns. His is already part of the sporting Camelot.

Age to age, old trees wither, young shoots blossom.
The laws of nature try to impose their rules but
athletes are now cheeking them at both ends of the
spectrum. Particularly on the younger side. Especially
in tennis.

Sugar, spice and all things nice
July 1st 1990

Spring flowers are the sweetest but they never last till summertime. Jennifer Capriati didn't just captivate Wimbledon last week, she made you long to change the present laws of tennis nature.

Court 2 is called "The Graveyard" but for those of us having a first complete match of the Capriati experience on Friday the place was more like a cradle. Out of it, after two and a half hours of sometimes indifferent but ultimately quite marvellously stirring play, came this charming, buck-toothed infant who misses her puppy back home in Wesley Chapel, Florida. She's just 14, for heaven's sake. Where on earth will it lead us?

The early answers are the easy ones. Tomorrow Capriati will play Steffi Graf in the first of what will become many highly paid, much-awaited encounters. In the opening months and years ahead Capriati's astonishing gifts will see her climb swiftly up the rankings and her seven-figure earnings will aim for the stratosphere. But look what happened to the comet.

In particular, recall the fate of other child prodigies who once had us drooling. On Thursday Capriati had made a first happy, smiling visit to Court 2 as part of a winning doubles team. Opposing her was Mrs Carling Bassett-Seguso, the "Darling Carling" of yesteryear, and one look could tell Capriati that fame can be a torturous friend.

In many ways Bassett-Seguso is out the other side. She is wife to doubles ace Robert Seguso and mother of his son. She is a beautifully dressed, elegant young lady but on Thursday on the tennis court her nerves were shot through. There were dark shadows under the eyes, a worried twitch in those frail stork-like arms as she tried to remember dreams of other days. It is not all easy in adulthood.

But at least Bassett-Seguso is able to play. The gloomiest thought that

So good but so young. Jennifer Capriati winning at Wimbledon in 1990. She was still only 14! (Norman Lomax)

keeps knocking on the door is the physical tithe that tennis is bound to seek. Tracy Austin's back and Andrea Jeager's hips now fascinate the X-ray libraries, not the Centre Court. How can Capriati's young body possibly survive the attrition that has to come?

Naturally her parents and coaches all claim to be very aware of the burn-out problem, to be very proud of their girl both as a player and as a person. From what we saw on Friday they have every right to be and it is good to know that Chris Evert has been close to the Capriati act. For although she had her share of injuries by the end, Chrissie's physique handled the relentless demands of the tennis treadmill just as her personality did the popping lamps of the paparazzi.

Yet even that comparison is far from exact. Evert wasn't in the Wimbledon fourth round as a 14-year-old and, crucially, people didn't immediately talk of hers as a highly physical game. Witness opponent Robin White in the interview room on Friday: "Steffi Graf may be the better athlete but Jennifer is remarkable in how hard she hits the ball, and the way she keeps going."

It is one thing to say that a 14-year-old has precocious skills with which to dazzle her seniors, quite another to state that part of her success depends on power and fitness at a time when the body is still a long way short of maturity. Worse, it is one thing to revel in Capriati's wonderfully unselfconscious charm, another to realise that multi-million-pound sponsorship deals are already linked to it.

As she pigeon-toed on to court on Friday she was a unique mixture of mammon and maidenhood. She had her head bowed but her face could not suppress a "gee, ain't this great" grin which brought a glow to all of us in the sunshine, and no doubt to those moguls who have paid vast sums for the rights to her racket, clothes and for the signature across the side of the shoes. "Heck," said Martina Navratilova earlier in the week, "I am 31 years of age and I haven't had a shoe named after me yet."

Part of the attraction is in the freshness, in the sheer novelty value of the Capriati show. And for a time on Friday it was hard to avoid an echo of Dr Johnson's famous chauvinism about a woman preaching being like a dog walking on its hind legs. It is not that she does it well but that she does it at all which is of interest.

Capriati was down 0-2 in the first and second sets, down 0-3 in the third after that extraordinary 32-point game which looked to have finished her. There were moments when she would net an easy return or over-hit one of her ambitious drives, the already famous grunt would become a little desperate and the crowd would sigh with sympathy rather than sizzle with delight.

Up against her, 26-year-old White, with her bleach-blonde hair and rolling sailor's walk, looked like some stern Californian gym mistress. But Miss White's nice smile took on a grim line in scowls as she failed to put away the winners, and across the net the dream took flight.

Forget all the cutie charm, forget even what may lie ahead. The real significance of Friday was that this, for Wimbledon, was the first time. The first time that Capriati had (since her match started at 12.30) been centre stage. The first time that many of us had seen that whipped, laser-accurate, double-fisted backhand, and had watched that astonishing imperturbability under pressure.

When a match comes alive, it becomes a shared experience. Suddenly in that third set the chatter from the players' balcony was hushed, and as the young phenomenon took charge for that final six-game winning streak it was even as if the old church on the hill had turned round to look.

Afterwards in the interview room, the laughing brown eyes no longer slitted with concentration, here was a lovely young girl who had just won the school prize. One of us asked a ponderous question about the pressure of waiting two days for the confrontation with Graf. "I guess I may get a little impatient," said Capriati, wanting to agree but not quite getting the point of nervous anticipation. "Gee, I am looking forward to playing her so much."

Who knows what the future holds? Spring flowers may not last. But let's treasure them while we can.

Predictions are easier when you get to sunset time. You know where they are going, it's just the exact schedule you aren't certain of. And the greater they are, the longer the delay.

Nonetheless there is a sadness about decline. And when you have come to St Andrews, "the auld toun" almost Mediterranean in the July heat, the Old Course a shimmering green. When you are lucky enough to be on the inside ropes of the greatest golf tournament of them all. When you watch Jack Nicklaus in the Open. You feel it.

Golden Bear gets no mercy from the Old Lady
July 22nd 1990

Like great ships they passed, Faldo and Norman eager and outward bound, but for Nicklaus trudging up the fifteenth fairway it was as if evening had come.

Jack Nicklaus doesn't owe golf anything. The massive debt is entirely the other way round, so it was sad to see him suffer as the sun beat down on the Old Course where for so long he has been the man they had to beat.

Not a putt would sink. Again and again they would hang on the very lip. Just one birdie in a round played in perfect conditions, five shots dropped, cruelly including the last three holes for a final score of 77. That great Roman brow would never ask for mercy and yesterday "The Old Lady" was never granting it.

Of course all the charisma is still there and the "Golden Bear" carries history with him. Fathers push sons forward to try and touch him coming through. He may not be hitting the scoreboard but the day is not complete without his presence. But Nicklaus could never settle for just an easy exhibition round. True, he has the most regal of all those crowd-acknowledging waves, but he was here to play golf.

That meant the practice tee long before noon. The famous bronzed face and flaxen hair atop navy blue sweater, maroon trousers and white shoes as if he had just dropped off from a yachting holiday in Cape Cod.

From practice tee to putting green in that zoo-like pen beneath the grandstand. The touch looks marvellously sure but the balls didn't sink

Opposite: Age is the enemy. Jack Nicklaus facing up to the passing of the years (Chris Smith)

and you notice a long line in the Nicklaus cheek when his head dipped in concentration.

He was playing with Ronan Rafferty, Europe's top player in 1989 and a man whose massive forearms threaten to set any course aflame. No such thoughts soup up the simplicity of the playing announcement: "On the tee, Ronan Rafferty."

The big Irishman smashes his drive a long way down the fairway, then the greatest golfer of his age steps again on to centre stage at St Andrews and we get the absolute opposite of those Las Vegas pre-fight "champion of the world, the one and only" announcements. A quiet Scottish voice intones politely, "On the tee, Jack Nicklaus."

A wave of applause breaks out, but it is full more of affection than expectation and straight away they are proved right. Nicklaus' tee shot finds its way into the burn. The omens aren't good.

Most of us now watch golf on television—which, through marvellous editing and commentary, takes us unerringly to the crises and climaxes as they develop. In reality, even at St Andrews, with the sun out and the town resplendent in the distance, it is not like that. For most matches it's a long four hours of struggle with a sense of yearning for that magic touch and in Nicklaus' case, for yesteryear.

He can still play the shots. After that setback at the first, he came close to birdies three times before finally pulling a shot back at the fifth. But the longer the match went on, the more certain you felt that there would be none of those remote-control putts that strangle the crowd's breath and then release it in a roar of applause.

Again and again father and son would make an anguished family study, Jackie caddying for his dad as they lined up the shots together. Only once did the iron control break. On the short eighth there was a chance of a birdie two. The ball ran past. "No, I missed it," called out Nicklaus senior. Even the gods grow old. As an answer Jack turned to bananas, munching one enthusiastically as he marched up the ninth with another birdie chance. That wouldn't drop either.

Then it began to go properly wrong. Three putts at both the 10th and 11th and, in the invidious comparisons that St Andrews' famous "loop" imposes, these coincided with great explosions of applause as Ian Baker-Finch tore up the course one match after Nicklaus and Rafferty. The score board showed two over for the day, Baker-Finch nine under and now heading up the leader board.

Nicklaus looked across at the tall, reed-thin figure of Baker-Finch with interest. He had been there so many times in other days. He and Rafferty were on the long road home and the Irishman had no magic either.

Woosnam came past, a round little figure dressed in grey but full of purpose. Then Payne Stewart, dressed in what looked like yellow and blue offcuts from the sail locker, then Norman and Faldo. The others had the battles and the headlines to seek.

Nicklaus just had to get home safely. He couldn't do it. A good drive over the hotel at the 17th and then a long-looking second.

"Good shot," said some flathead in the crowd, but the ball found the bunker just the same.

At 50, Jack could settle for appearances on the senior tour. He will always be honoured whenever talk turns to golf. But he is a proud man. Something tells you the ship is not aiming for the harbour yet.

From "slow twitch" to "fast twitch". It may take more than 3 hours to complete a round of the Open, but it is only 13 seconds from gun to line in the 110 metres hurdles. It's a concentration of mind and muscle as tight and pure as they come. Colin Jackson was the best in Britain. He was tilting at the world itself. He has his own ways of priming the pump.

Joy, fun, and seasons in the sun
July 22nd 1990

It was a full hour into the training session when something almost surprising happened. Colin Jackson actually broke into a jog. Was the big black cat at last ready to spring?

Not yet he wasn't. After no more than 50 yards of dainty, almost mincing steps, Jackson's new burst of activity was over. Wales' most likely entry for Man of the Nineties turned, ambled back to the start line and stretched out again beside his team-mates.

Sure, it was hot in Cardiff on Wednesday, even at six o'clock in the evening. But this seemed hardly enough to strain a caterpillar. Here was a clutch of the best high hurdlers in the world under the very nose of their distinguished coach, Malcolm Arnold, giving a fair imitation of having a good time. And here was Jackson, supposedly beset by a blip in form and by a controversy about leaving his club and forming some new élite group for top athletes, apparently uninterested in anything more than whose drinks bottle he could pinch from the kit-locker.

"It's all true," Jackson said, his smiling Welsh voice coming as a contrast to the utterly Caribbean rhythms of his general demeanour. "We really enjoy ourselves in this group. We have so much fun that people think we don't train seriously. But when they see us laughing they don't take into account the work we do.

"Not much quantity, I admit." His head comes forward and his hands go wide as he jokes, unable to keep up the serious vein beyond the 13 seconds it takes for those rocketing 110-metre shoot-outs. "But the work is very high quality. When others try and join us, they soon understand."

The diamond of Jackson's talent is so flashy that at times you want to doubt the quality of the carbon at its heart. For this is a young man of quite remarkable physical beauty. His 5ft 11in, 12st 4lb frame has been honed to a muscular blend of power and grace that can match anything in the animal kingdom. And at 23 his personality is still sunshine almost all the way. If his head is for turning, it ought to be spinning by now.

The list of achievements is already long enough to crowd out the scrap books his Jamaican father, "Ossie" Jackson, lovingly keeps at the family home in Birch Grove, Cardiff. Gold medal in the World Junior Championships, gold in the European Indoors, gold this January in the Commonwealth, silver in the Olympics.

Although the great Roger Kingdom remains the world No. 1, Jackson is ready not just to take him on but to capture his world record into the bargain. Kingdom and Renaldo Nehemiah have been the only two men legally to break the magic 13-second barrier. Jackson has been there twice already, albeit with the aid of an excess breeze.

Jackson in full flood is fast developing into one of the most recognisable images of the present scene. The long fingers spread wide on the start line. Those eight biting, arm-pumping strides up to the first hurdle and then the lightning three-stride rhythm, right through the breath-busting 10-hurdle sequence. Nobody, not even the powerhouse Roger Kingdom, does it with such panache.

The brilliance was there from the beginning. At Llanederyn High School, Jackson was devastating at any discipline he tried and at 14 he had a Saturday when a call from junior county cricket clashed with representing Cardiff in track and field. "I tossed a coin," he remembered, "it came down for track and field, and you know I finished only fourth. But that was one of the big decisions." Another was the switch to hurdling. "I used to do javelin, high jump, long jump, everything bar the hurdles," said Jackson. "Then one day the teacher said, 'We'll do some hurdles today,' and it was really easy. I liked the idea. It would save me long jumping—no sand in my shoes. And I wouldn't hurt my shoulder doing the javelin. It was easy and allowed me to spring. I could already run fast."

That, at least, is Jackson's throwaway version of the story. Malcolm Arnold, who coaxed the Ugandan policeman John Akii-Bua to 400m hurdles gold in the 1972 Olympics, has a more measured recall. "Even up till Colin won the World Junior Championships in 1986, there was real thought of the long jump or the decathlon. He was such a talented all-round athlete—but once he'd won a world championship, the decision wasn't difficult."

It soon becomes clear that while Jackson may not want to be serious, he takes his sport earnestly enough. "His physical talent is obvious," Arnold continued, looking across to where Jackson was now beginning a short, shunting, high-stepping burst past the overturned hurdles, "but he commits himself. He regulates his life. Compare him now and before a race, and he's a different person."

So the most crucial of all the decisions was when, at 18, Colin decided to opt out of all work experience schemes and go for full-time athletics. His parents were against it. "Ossie" is a service supervisor with the Caerphilly firm of Nu-Aire and his mother is a nurse who leaves the best reggae-backed message on any answering machine this side of the water. They aren't against it now. Their little boy is getting even more famous than his sister, Suzanne, an actress in Channel 4's *Brookside*.

Back to Wednesday evening, and a more businesslike mood took hold as the purpose of the earlier hour's cat exercises emerged. Jackson and the other hurdlers were now interspersing their high-stepping hackney trots with contortions of the lower limbs you wouldn't see outside the circus. You certainly don't start doing that sort of thing without first tweaking every muscle to the very limit of its elasticity.

It's a cosmopolitan team that begins to fiddle with the starting blocks. There's Nigel Walker, the British champion before Jackson came through to take his title and to repair a once-strained relationship. There's Kay Morley, the primary school teacher who won gold in Auckland. There's a junior championship contender, Paul Gray. There's a visiting West Indian called Yves McDavid (his horse-mad father wanted to commemorate the visit of the French jockey Yves Saint-Martin to Barbados). And, more controversially, there's Jackson's house guest, the Canadian Mark McKoy.

The raised eyebrow is because McKoy was part of the same muscle-pumped training set-up which produced Ben Johnson at the last Olympics. Nothing was ever proved, but McKoy left Seoul in a hurry. Even a practically rehabilitated Johnson hardly seems the right sort of stablemate for someone like Jackson, who has never touched alcohol, let alone steroid syringes, and who is currently participating in an anti-doping video.

Jackson didn't try to skirt round this particular hurdle. "Mark was part of the Ben Johnson team," he said. "He was taking the things, but he's okay now. He's slimmer, but he's running really quick. He regrets doing it. It's in the past." Certainly McKoy was carrying none of the unnatural muscle bulk on Wednesday which so marked Johnson in Seoul. With a small, mean moustache atop a stubbled chin, a hard-muscled torso and black Tour de France shorts, McKoy looked every inch the racer—and it was he who first took the eye when Malcolm Arnold finally called the team to the line.

In this first series, the race was just to the first hurdle. Up on the blocks, reaction, eight pumping strides to take-off, then a strange out-of-gear slow-down through the flattened second hurdle and just about needing to push over the third before coming to a halt.

With so much emphasis on reaction time, little wonder that, to begin with, concentration was faulty. The spanking new grandstand might be gleaming under the lowering sun, but Malcolm Arnold's "pistol" was simply the smack of his two hands clapped together. Four times he slapped them again for the "false start" call, the last time prompting Kay Morley to exclaim, "Oh, come on!" as if some wretched infant had done something really dreadful at the back of the class.

But once the runners got the act together, it was McKoy who made the first mark. Twice he was decisively quicker off his blocks, and as Malcolm Arnold watched him freewheel to a halt at the third hurdle, he turned, slashed the air with his hands and said with a fan's fervour: "That Mark McKoy, he was out like a bullet."

Did this praise mean any lessening of the belief in Master Jackson, who had not at this point recaptured his peak form since last month's final hurdle crash in his most recent duel with Roger Kingdom? "No," Malcolm said decisively. "The peak needs to be the middle of August—Roger Kingdom in the Zurich Grand Prix, and then the European Championships in Split.

"At the moment, Colin has one or two problems. Hurdling is a series of individual skills as you go down the track. If you get one thing wrong, more and more goes wrong. At Belfast on Monday [where Jackson only just held off the young pretender Tony Jarrett] you could see that he was a bit off-balance coming away from his hurdles. But he's a very perceptive athlete and he'll put it right."

Earlier, Jackson had done one of his switches from self-mockery ("My school report said I should try harder in all aspects except talking") to real intensity. "I did have a lovely hurdling style," he said, "but it's not so good now. When I fell I slightly twisted my hip, and in my next races to compensate for the hip I changed my technique a bit. Then the hip got better, but the technique didn't. I'm in perfect shape, the right racing weight. I'm sprinting quick, a 100-metre personal best on 10.49. It's just that I can't hurdle."

As he talked, the significance of all other questions seemed to pale. The problems at Cardiff were dismissed in little more than a sentence: "I don't like hassle, so rather than have hassle I leave." The new scheme is very much in the embryonic stage. "It's only an idea at the moment," he said. "We haven't sat down with all the athletes yet. It's mainly an educational thing, to go to the schools, to get the kids interested, to spread the word for athletics."

Hard though it may be for some of us old cynics to believe it, what really sparks Colin Jackson is the thing itself. He may have a new Sierra Sapphire,

a three-bedroomed house and a six-figure sum in his trust fund. He may be one of the best-looking men on the planet, but what he wants is to become the fastest two-legged creature ever to run at a hurdle in anger.

There is no obvious anger out on the track now, but the session, like the season, is building to a climax. You remember Arnold's single biggest compliment: "Colin has a tremendous ability to concentrate when it matters, an innate ability to go up a gear."

"You have to pull yourself together on the big occasions," Jackson had said. The pauses between jokes were getting long, the face more often assuming the mask we recognise on race day. "But I also believe that what will be, will be—there's no point in worrying. There's been no problem, not even the Olympics."

We had come to the final stage of the evening—and middle-distance runners whose training schedules involve scores of miles a week might respond with a snort of "big deal". This lot have never even jogged more than 100 yards, and now they were into tonight's maximum trip—a run-up and then four hurdles. Just 50 metres of effort.

But this was serious. The last T-shirt was stripped off and you could see where the intensive sessions of weight training had given power across the

The body beautiful. Colin Jackson getting changed for action in Cardiff (Adam Scott)

175

pectorals. Kay Morley was lined up a lane apart from the men, the smaller women's hurdles ahead of her, but the concentration no less intensive.

At the first start it was again McKoy who broke best. Jackson's sinew-packed blue shorts brushed down the first hurdle but by the time they came past us he, McKoy and Walker were almost level.

One tubby club athlete was still puffing—sweaty, alone and helpless—around the empty track. The distant noise of the dual carriageway into Cardiff blended with sheep-bleat and seagull-cry. The athletes walked back, that loose amble now a much more assertive strut, their bodies arrogant with self-belief.

Malcolm Arnold held them on their blocks. A white-haired figure with the stomach of middle age, he raised his palms aloft like a priest at the altar. The comparison was not inexact: the five men and one woman had only got to those starting blocks through a dedication almost akin to religious faith. "There may be money in it now," Jackson had said, "but you only continue with athletics if you really love it."

The white hands clapped together. The black limbs drove furiously into life. This time Colin Jackson did not miss the cue. Those same eight biting strides up to that flowing, leg-splitting leap. Three more strides, still on the roll to the next leap. Three more and he was coming towards us, the others already adrift and his body working with a deadly liquid grace that may one day sign off in history.

As he took the fourth hurdle there had been just 17 strides of effort, but what we had seen was seared into the memory. So, too, were his words from earlier in the day. "All the training," he had said, "is to try and pinpoint the tiny things that will finally make me the perfect hurdler. It's the incentive to train harder, when you see that you could be supreme."

There are big rewards now for the sacrifices he makes, but calling them sacrifices misses the point. For a few short summers he is fashioning mind and body for the ultimate. And, unless eyes deceive, he is having the time of his life.

As he strode back after that dazzling final run, he put his hands on his hips and turned to Nigel Walker, his eyes wide with delight. "Boy," Colin Jackson said, sucking in a deep breath of satisfaction. "I had a living start."

Colin Jackson has not quite made it to World No.1 but he has time on his side. Not so our last two portraits. Both of them had surely gone the other side of prime. But neither of them were counting on it. Steve Davis was "interested" in the experience of defeat but eager to get the habit of winning again. Bryan Robson? In the autumn of 1990, the question marks had been wheeled out in bigger shape than ever.

Happy, hungry and ready for more
August 19th 1990

He is already history. It's to the video shelf that we turn to see the best of Bryan Robson. Or could our hero still treat us to yet another chapter?

The omens are not good. "Of course he'll never play for England again," said the Heathrow baggage checker on Thursday. He would know. "I have to think he's peaked," said Alan Ball on Friday. "He's been a great player but he seems to be on the wane." With 72 England caps, a World Cup Winner's medal and a career which lasted until he was 38, Ball just might know.

But actually we all think we know. For it's true to say that, over the last 10 years, few careers in the whole of British life have attracted such interest, admiration and affection as that of Robson. He's given us everything we could want in a people's hero. He's had the ultimate success but remained an ordinary guy, the captain who led from the front but paid the price. Often the strongest feeling for him has been one of sympathy.

Now we are at it again. As he limped off in the second half of the World Cup match against The Netherlands in June, even the optimists had to think it was over. In the previous World Cup it was the dislocated shoulder. There have been broken legs, smashed noses and torn hamstrings so frequent that "New Robson Injury Crisis" is the one headline that every paper seems to have permanently set.

This time, surely, there can be no wonder comeback for "Captain Marvel". He was 33 in January and begins his 18th First Division season with a six-inch scar up the sheath of his Achilles' tendon and an interrupted rehabilitation programme that still has a month to run. Going to his house this week was to relish the past, not to thrill over the future.

Beware assumptions, especially when so easy to make. The present Robson home fits splendidly into the "fruits of football" image. In the best of Cheshire suburbia, just 10 miles from Manchester airport, it is an imposing mock Tudor residence set back from wrought-iron railings and remote control front gates which open soundlessly while we pay the cab-driver. Inside, too, everything is the height of luxurious respectability. Panelled walls, unobtrusive oil paintings, a state-of-the-art kitchen, a snooker room, a sitting-room straight out of the Selfridges brochure; all so clean that a speck of dirt would offend as much as a bad back-pass to the goalkeeper.

The great man is still out training. Denise Robson brings us ground coffee in a glass jug. At last we see a photo of one of the most public men of our times. It stands neatly on a corner table. It is a family group taken this spring. Bryan wears a top hat. They are outside Buckingham Palace with his OBE.

It's the most understated ornament I have seen since (if you are going to drop names, drop them big) inspecting two little trophies on Omar Sharif's mantelpiece. They were the World Bridge Championship and the Oscar for *Doctor Zhivago*.

It's all so immaculate, so richly deserved that there can't surely be the same commitment to risk having your limbs rearranged every Saturday on the football field. Other ambitions, a manager's job, businesses, charities, we will understand, but to want to go charging out with "the lads" will surely sound like the old warrior whistling to himself for self-delusion, the fading maestro whose vanity blinds him to the truth.

First impressions are not too good. Despite some Graham Gooch-style designer stubble, Robson looks young and fresh enough in his grey slacks and pink tennis shirt, but then he reveals that there was a setback last week. "It flared up after my first big run," he explains. "I thought I would have to have another operation. I went to Harley Street and they gave me these tablets and a stretching routine and it seems better now."

There is the obligatory pulling up of the left trouser leg and the examination of the most important scar in football. "They made an incision there at the back of the Achilles' tendon," he says. "They had four or five blood clots to scrape away. When the sheath grows back you get some thickening. I got a little more than I should have done, some inflammation."

It is all said very matter-of-factly but your first thought is to ring Ladbrokes to extend the odds about the comeback. Yet while Robson is almost shy and unfailingly polite (in three hours the only time he uses a four-letter word is to describe an ex-international prone to well-paid attacks on the England management), there is still an infectious certainty about him. Those big brown eyes don't look away from you. Robson doesn't need to boast.

"At Manchester United we have the best physio in football, Jim MacGregor. I put a lot of my recoveries down to him. He knows exactly how long to rest and what treatment to get you running again. I had a long hard run yesterday, and another this morning and, touch wood, it feels fine. We should be in business next month."

But how good a business? It is 10 years since he first pulled on an England shirt. Those surging runs, those wonderfully timed tackles that he completes with a pass, that never-failing courage—surely the blunting must come soon? Especially with the accumulation of injuries and, let's say it, with the well-known thirst which sees him on his second driving ban?

There's a smile, and the Geordie accent, diluted by having left home at 15 for West Brom, returns thicker when he says, "I will always hold my hand up and say I am a drinker. But I have a golden rule not to drink two nights before a game. Sometimes I don't have a drink for a week but I like the social side of it. It definitely relaxes you. I have never felt I have missed out on life.

*Captain Marvel.
With Bryan Robson
the nickname was
almost an
understatement
(Chris Smith)*

"Mind you, I am lucky," he adds with the touch of gratitude that adorns his conversation. "I can eat or drink anything and not put on weight. Even after a skinful I don't have a hangover and can still be up in front with the others. When I fall back in the pack I will know the legs are telling me something."

A day later Alan Ball remembered getting the message. "It's like death, it comes real quick," he said. "But before it comes you can use your knowledge to cut the pitch down. Robson might have to limit those runs of his to just two or three a half, but he has such vast experience that he could still play marvellously at the back."

There seems to be some sort of consensus of hope in football circles that a sweeper's role might give us some borrowed time for Robson. For the man himself it is not exactly a "world exclusive" idea. "I played there in the youth team," he says, and he is happy to try it again. "I get great satisfaction out of playing in defence. People get carried away with the fact that it's only when a player beats a player or scores a goal that it's skill. Tackling is very much a skill of the game as well.

"That's why I think England have a great chance. For with Mark Wright, Paul Parker and Des Walker we have an absolutely first-class defence. We just have to get the goalscoring side a bit slicker with Gary Lineker, Paul Gascoigne and David Platt. All through my years I have never met a player as skilful as Paul Gascoigne."

But hadn't the Heathrow baggage handler, let alone the man on the Clapham omnibus, said that Robson's England days were over? "I quite like the challenge of being written off," he says. You notice that the cheeks are quite round and boyish but the eyes are very direct again. "When I spoke to Graham Taylor, I said my ambition was to qualify and win the European Championship in two years' time. I think we have the players and I want to be part of it."

Yet what of domestic football, another season, another round of local derbies, top-of-the-table cliff-hangers and cup-ties? With the house, the burgeoning business interests under the ubiquitous Harry Swales, with the arrival of baby Ben to complement Clare and Charlotte who have just come back, all dusty-jodhpured, from the morning riding class, surely some of the need, the hunger must have gone?

"I think football is just as important to me," he says directly. "Perhaps it helps not having won the championship. Every team sets off to win the league. We got a lot of stick last season but ended up winning the FA Cup. We have some fine young players, Lee Sharp, Lee Martin, Russell Beardsmore, Mark Robins. I would love all of them to come out and prove themselves. Then I know that it's going to make my job easier to win the championship. I really began to think it was happening at the end of last season."

Suddenly the listener is into the rarest of privileges, sitting with one of the great masters of a profession as the conversation takes flight. The fascination of captaincy: "Trying to keep the shape of the team"; the improvement in training techniques: "Everyone is much fitter nowadays, not just in work, but in knowledge of diet and rest"; of great players, and of how it all began: "I have always had confidence in myself to play football. I joined the scouts solely because they had a football team which was in the semi-final."

It is now well told how the lorry driver's son from Chester-le-Street in Co Durham got signed up by West Brom as a 7st weakling, but that early immaturity and what was needed to overcome it provide some of the best ammunition for hopes of an Indian summer.

"People's bodies are definitely different," Robson says. "I remember Ray Wilkins at 15. He had a great hairy chest and was the shape he is now. I have put on four stone since then. And the fact that I have missed quite a lot through injury, the whole of the '76–77 season, has made me realise what I have missed, made me keener."

There are lovely cameos of the emerging star. "One day at Coventry, West Brom were two up after 20 minutes and Len Cantello turned to me and said, 'If you keep going like this you will play for England.' I had never thought of it before." There are tributes to other players. Terry McDermott: "I used to be just a blaster, he had so many different ways of scoring goals"; Frank Stapleton: "He was a terror for extra heading practice. I used to stay behind with him. It was fun and developed the skill."

He gets up to go and fetch some more coffee. That walk, toes slightly in, no swagger but very certain. We've all marched behind it out into the great stadia of the world. What was the best match of all? Old question but an answer warmed by the memory. "It has to be that first World Cup match against France in 1982. They had Platini, he's the best I've ever seen. I thought it was a real challenge for me, and to get that first goal so quick and then another in the second half, that was about perfect."

What about the worst match? He likes that question. "Leicester, for West Brom," he says with an instant smile. "The only time I have been substituted. What was wrong? I was absolute crap. I told the manager he was quite right and he should have taken me off earlier."

So what happens after the final whistle? "I've no strategy," he says calmly. "I just weigh the situation up at the end of each season. It looks as if I will go on to being a manager but it depends on what jobs come up. But I will not be going into the Third or Fourth Division. I've not played there and don't know about organising those teams."

We are on to the future and it doesn't seem to hurt. "I know enough about the Second and First Division teams to be a successful manager there, but the only problem is I'm not going to be the manager of a club who can't get a decent crowd. I don't want to build up a team and then be told to sell players to get some money. I can't work like that so it cuts the field down a bit."

Although he doesn't mention it, and while he obviously holds considerable admiration for Alex Ferguson, all of the above doesn't preclude many United fans' dream that Robson may one day be persuaded to do a Kenny Dalglish and succeed Ferguson to the managerial chair at Old Trafford. That ought to be just about the most significant journalistic question, yet it is a long way behind the central one. What fuels the drive in Robson? Of course one afternoon is only a peep through the window of someone's life but it's easy to over-complicate. There are no secrets about Bryan Robson. He has a wonderful natural talent, he has worked at it and is grateful for it. Put on the spot for an epitaph, he says: "I just want them to think, 'He always gave 100 per cent.' "

Yet there is another witness we should call. Bryan Robson senior still lives in Chester-le-Street, in the same council house in which he and Maureen raised Bryan, Susan, Justin and Gary. All three boys have played First Division football. Justin retired early from Newcastle with a bad knee injury, Gary is with West Brom.

On Wednesday Bryan junior will be going to York to follow his love of racing (he currently has three horses in training). Bryan senior will be going slightly further afield. Sixty years old, and in his 33rd year with the same firm, he will be driving a 38-ton Volvo truck to Germany. Don't tell him about early retirement.

When England's captain first got some money he suggested he might buy the council house for his parents. "Dad said, 'I will buy it my bloody self.'" On Friday Bryan senior chuckled gently at the story and said: "Well, what I really told him was that I was quite comfortable but if he didn't look after our Mam and the others when I was gone I would come back and haunt him."

Bryan Robson senior had trials for both Sunderland and Newcastle, and his father was a famous left-half for a team called Chester Thespians. His memories go back to his son's schooldays when masters first said that "our Bryan" was "outstanding".

Listening to him and to his son on the eve of a new season made you remember other words at another time. Looked at the Robson way it can again be what Pele called it, "the beautiful game".

Two days after that interview the Achilles' tendon needed another operation and it was not until December that he played again. But he worked his way back into the Manchester United and, albeit temporarily, into the England side. For Steve Davis, at the time of writing, the tide has still not turned.

Can he cope with being second best?
December 16th 1990

The loser's interview. A shattered player trying to put a brave face on things. A scuffle of pressmen plugging variations of the old question, "What went wrong?" On Thursday, it happened to Steve Davis. Again.

The Brentwood Leisure Centre on an icy December night is quite a long way from Acapulco. And while the World Matchplay looks glamorous enough on the box, what passes for the press room is no more than a little bare-bricked office at the end of the gallery. But off the table there are no frills on Steve Davis. Not on Thursday, not as a loser.

It's a good job snooker doesn't stand too heavy on its own dignity. "Where's Davis? In the dope test?" asks a voice over the shoulder of Stephen Hendry who is perched on a wooden chair in the midst of us deadline-hurried hacks. The ubiquitous hutch mother of the snooker scribblers, her head covered by huge radio earphones, is already into her report.

"It was the pink in the 13th frame that proved the downfall of Davis . . ." The voice rattled on; a camera and microphone were stuck in front of Hendry. Davis would come later.

Six defeats in a row to Hendry is pretty conclusive, even more so for someone who through the eighties took success to a point of boring invincibility. Hendry, not 22 until next month, acknowledges Davis's decline. "I don't think Steve is playing as well as he was five years ago," he says in a crisp Scottish voice occasionally made soggy with flu. "But that may have a lot to do with me beating him."

Snooker is full of such profundities, the simplest and yet deepest of games which through its addictive TV appeal seems to take us up the cue into the very minds of the players. Now we have to cope with Steve Davis as a loser.

In other sports defeat often brings with it a wall of silence, but not in snooker. Not with promoter Barry Hearn sitting with his winner's smile in the hospitality suite. Not, most of all, with Steve Davis. He has a black leather bomber jacket over the silk playing waistcoat and he faces the questions head on. "It's disappointing to lose," he says, thinking through his answer. "But I am fighting, and the fact that I am fighting is proof that I am getting involved and that's important because I want to stay in the game."

Deadlines are pressing. Right beside him one reporter is bellowing a story down the line, yet Davis continues. At 33 he is still heron-thin but at this time of night the bags under the eyes are beginning to show the strain of having spent a decade at the top. He makes a virtue of his new position. "I am quite enjoying this feeling of having to work for things. I feel as if I am in with a shout against Stephen now. I am enjoying the process of putting my game together. I just need to win a tournament."

Can he, in the words of a far less gracious superstar, really "be serious"? Can he really enjoy those moments when the magic suddenly goes, when the spell he seems to have put on the table suddenly evaporates, when the ball, inexplicably, insultingly, refuses to sink?

Two such moments remain vivid from the three hours of the closing session of that semi-final. The first in the 10th frame. Davis in charge, takes the blue but comes up short on the pink. He will have to pot hard to get the cue ball round to the black. There is almost violence in the force of the shot. There is a gasp of mortality when the pink judders round and then out of the pocket while the cue ball rockets off on the diagonal and almost drops at the other end.

Worst of all was the pink in the 13th frame. Davis had battled back to square things six-all at the interval and after being snookered up the far corner got the cue ball away out the other end of the table. Not away enough. At moments like this Hendry's lower lip bulges in concentration. It had been like that in the 10th. As then, the shot was hard, and fast, and ruthless. In the silence the noise as the pink crashed into the pocket was as triumphant as a clash of cymbals.

We have got so used to the Davis face in victory that we now become fascinated by it in defeat. It's as if some great certainty has left us.

"It's quite funny really," Davis had said the day before back in his heartland at Romford, "despite a couple of mediocre performances early this season I have justified my position as No. 2 in the world which is not exactly disastrous." He was talking in Barry Hearn's hyperactive but unpretentious headquarters off Romford High Street. Packing cases crowd the reception desks, telephones ring, the odd track-suited fighter shadow-boxes in a corner. Barry Hearn himself sits upstairs in a meeting, a huge unopened magnum of champagne on the table.

Davis plays it completely unflash. "The one bad thing about being well known," he says, "is having to dress smart. Away from the snooker table I am just a slob."

On this day he was dressed in a blue track suit, grey sweat-shirt and very white trainers where we normally see those black patent leather pumps. He is bigger and stronger-looking than you expect and, contrary to his Spitting Image persona, he is a witty and observant companion. He has the great virtue among megastars of having come to terms—rather than of being obsessed—with himself.

"One thing I have found about Stephen's success," he says with a wry grin, "is that people act more positively to me. They don't see me as such

The master cueman. Steve Davis was metronomically unbeatable in the early days, but nothing is forever (Chris Smith)

a threat or a bighead. I used to bring out such a strong anti-feeling. It was as if they thought I was trying to be too clever and they were angry at their own failings."

Plenty of psychologists have already beaten their way to the Davis door to find the secret of his success or now the thrill of his comparative failure. He is marvellously dismissive of the heavy stuff. "I haven't got a clue what is inside my head," he says with a laugh. "I just do this because it's what I am good at."

That said, he admits to being into his third age as a snooker player. "The first is coming up through the ranks. I began to get attention at school so I worked at it. The second is making it to the top and being in the public eye. That is now satisfied and I have to ask the question, 'Do I like snooker for snooker's sake or just for what it can do for me?' The only way you can answer that is to ask whether you are prepared to practise."

On that score he is still clearly a contender. Over the road in the impressive-sounding but unstylish Matchroom Club, he was in the midst of his daily four-hour practice session with his father Bill Davis.

"The repetition of practice is the pride of keeping it up," he says, becoming almost lyrical. "Every shot is a problem. You have to think about what you are doing, going through the mechanics of the technique to get the shot in the pocket and getting on to the next ball which is the thinking process of the continuation of the positional play."

Nonetheless he admits to faults he has been working on, which only now put him "in with a shout" against the "Wonder Bairn" who has taken his title. "There were two things," he says. "For some time, until quite recently, I hadn't been happy with my practice technique. And secondly, I had started to gamble a bit too much on the table. It was against my natural style and I attribute it to giving up, to saying 'Oh hell. I am not playing very well, let's give it a go.'"

As he talks the professionalism floods through. "All psychology books miss the point. The truth is that you are lucky to have found something you are good at. Luckily I was good at snooker and I was lucky enough to realise that I had to work hard to become very good."

There are those who will say that his day is past, that he ought to replace his father with a proven coach like Frank Callan, that marriage and impending parenthood have sapped his desire. Davis dismisses such easy solutions but still faces up to what the years will bring. "Somewhere down the line," he says with no mystery in the London voice, "in the way nature works you are superseded by another load of players who are playing on a different plateau to you. All of a sudden you are going down and a lot of people are going up. I don't know what the feeling will be like to be a real failure at this game. To be an also-ran."

Those may sound like autumn thoughts but they were soon followed by a champion's credo. We are off through Romford's fairy lights and Christmas shoppers to where Bill Davis and three other mates wait at the practice table. "Of course, there's nothing like winning," said Davis over his shoulder. "Even though you love it, the reason you practise, the driving force, is winning. Winning a tournament is the tops. Playing well is not enough." Then with a big laugh, which hints at a mood which may yet wrest the title back from Hendry, he repeated himself. "Not nearly enough."

An ordinary man who has won extraordinary fame by doing an ordinary thing extraordinarily well. Davis still aims to be a killer, but nowadays he cannot hide the human touch. There was a moment on Thursday night that said it all.

It was even before he walked out of the huge darkened games area into the little, floodlit, audience-sandwiched, green-tabled cosmos where the World Matchplay Title was at stake. The announcer was about to go into the introductory routine: "A snooker legend . . . 51 major titles . . . six times world champion . . ." Those lucky enough to have got tickets were settling in for another round of the best match the game currently has on offer. Start time was scheduled for 7p.m. At five to Hendry and Davis come through the outer door and step into the shadows to the side of the playing area itself. Like thoroughbreds in the paddock they gleamed with preparation. Black silk figures, waistcoats tailored close, the long snooker cues the symbol of their calling. They stood apart. Hendry short and still. Davis tall, lean and pacing.

The public couldn't see them but you could sniff the expectation in the air. The greatest thing about snooker in the flesh is the total commitment of the audience. The cocoon of concentration is not confined to the players. The silence is so total that a stomach rumble is serious intrusion, a cough almost sacrilege. It is into this that the players must step. No one has ever cocooned himself as completely as Steve Davis who now pursed his lips below us.

He was to be announced first. He had moved up tense and ready for the entrance, then suddenly he walked back deep into the shadows and peered up to the hushed darkness of the gallery. He shielded his eyes, registered what he needed, and gave a wave of greeting. Two mates from the Matchroom, two of the lads who had been playing back in Romford the afternoon before, had got their passes for the match.

Whatever happens on the table, Steve Davis won't ever be a loser off it.

Despite all the privileges, all the access to famous names and unforgettable places, there is something of a "Dr Faustus come to judgement" about the sportswriter's deal.

Up to and during the event you are given quite

undeserved royal treatment. In Las Vegas there were white tigers caged in the hotel lobby. In South Africa they opened a game reserve early. In Munich they played other "games" especially late. And everywhere there was the ringside seat, the front row pass, the "drive-through" car sticker.

But afterwards, sometimes very immediately afterwards, you have to do your own particular deal with the devil. You have to write it down.

Nowhere is the exchange more certain than in the rugby internationals, and no instance more exact than the glorious, rain-scattered afternoon when England won the Grand Slam at Twickenham. One minute we were living one of the most overwhelming sporting moments of recent years, the next we were faced with a keyboard, a closing deadline, a sodden notebook and fingers too numb to do the typing.

It's at this stage that the wandering hack needs two things and needs them badly. He needs help from the already beleaguered specialist writers, and he needs a lot of luck. Thanks to the generosity of men like Steve Jones and Chris Rea the first has always been given. With this match the second came from a Gallic gentleman who sounded the trumpet when all seemed lost. In any case, this was the ultimate example of being privileged just to have been there. Let's hope we have paid some of the dues.

Power, passion and something *incroyable*
March 17th 1991

At the end they carried Will Carling above the shouting, above the crowd. He and his team can go into legend. They deserved their Grand Slam, but here they will always be remembered for beating the sublime.

For as long as people talk about this match—and it will live down the centuries—they will first talk about that extraordinary, stunning, unbelievable, breathtaking try by France. We had been promised moments of Blanco magic, but here he was, his opening touch, and the ball going the whole length of the stadium before Saint-André scored. It wasn't just *incroyable*. There wasn't a soul in the stadium who didn't bless themselves to be alive.

England won it. England were magnificent, relentless, brave, fast and true. But France made it. Made it by their brilliance. By that extraordinary potential that took us right down to the wire.

Several times it seemed as if England had the game rolled up. Despite that incredible riposte from France, by half-time they were well adrift as the England machine ground forward to 18-9. You even began to feel a bit sorry for *les tricolores* as they struggled with the rampaging English pack and Tachdijian looked as if he would need all his bandages to hold off Ackford through the line-out combat up ahead. He didn't last more than eight minutes before he had to limp off to the tunnel. The rain was coming, warm and steady and welcome. The French heads were dropping again as penalties came, arguments started and the score crept up to 21-13.

There was a great flow of confidence welling around the ground, flooding off the stands. With just 10 minutes left, Hodgkinson put a long kick forward direct to Sella. It was a chance for something *incroyable* again, the ball to spin through to Mesnel, Blanco and Lafond. But Sella, the great Sella, dropped it like a duffer and as he kicked it away in disgust you had to think the number was up.

It wasn't. Right as we began to get the watches ready, expectantly waiting for that final whistle, there was that rumbling lifting surge that put over the final French try, and when Camberabero kicked through that titanic conversion there was the heart-stopping realisation that all could yet be lost.

The French pack raced back to face the drop-out right in front of us, Roumat and Cabannes facing up furiously as Berbizier barked and harried at them for one more effort. Andrew put the ball right, Teague and Winterbottom hammered after it. White and blue shirts locked together in effort. Blanco hovered. It could still be stolen.

But justice was done. The last whistle. The crowd on the pitch. The players swallowed in the stampede. Concern that their iron discipline might finally go in their moment of triumph. But first Carling, then Hodgkinson were hoisted above the crowd. They saw each other across the tumult and punched the air in exultation. They had lived the day, had lived the season.

So have all of us lucky enough to follow them. They have given us the gamut of emotions. Controversy with the dreary pragmatism of the victory in Cardiff. Relief in the drilled professionalism of the Calcutta Cup. Passion with that final slogging triumph in Dublin. And now a match to burn long and warm in the memory.

Rugby has to have force and commitment, passion and power. Tempers will fray, mistakes will be made. But when it all works you end with a sense of gratitude. That feeling that two teams have taken themselves and you into a deep dramatic involvement you get nowhere else in sport.

It was like that yesterday. As good a finale as you could ask for. England's grand old policemen doing sterling service yet again. Andrew so sure and

brave. Some of the crowd may have made ugly noises when he was late-tackled by Cabannes but Andrew didn't. The controlling pattern of the English pack, the brilliant thrusts of Carling and Guscott, the rocketing speed of Heslop and Underwood, his side's only try-scorer.

Yet they needed something extra to bring the greatness out of them and yesterday they got it. The Five Nations Championship will not see Blanco again. But for as long as it is played they will talk of the try he started here. Blanco inside his own line, the gathering greyhound, across-pitch gallop before the pass to Sella. On to Camberabero. The kick ahead. The running catch. The second kick. The lurking, unmarked Saint-André stooping in to score. Rugby men will recite it down the ages.

As the sodden crowd drifted merrily away one *tricolore*-draped French fan produced a trumpet from inside his coat, turned towards us and blew a flawless version of "Auld Lang Syne". It was that sort of day.

The grandest slam. England forwards (from left) Mike Teague, Dean Richards and Wade Dooley, the head of the juggernaut (Chris Smith)

Index

Name entries in italic refer to names of horses.
Page numbers in italic denote illustrations